LIBRARY ASSISTANCE TO READERS

By the Same Author

BIBLIOGRAPHIES, SUBJECT AND NATIONAL

DICTIONARIES OF FOREIGN LANGUAGES

INFORMATION SERVICES

INDEXES AND INDEXING

MODERN STORAGE EQUIPMENT AND METHODS FOR

SPECIAL MATERIALS IN LIBRARIES

THE TREATMENT OF SPECIAL MATERIAL IN LIBRARIES

BOOK COLLECTING

NEWNES DICTIONARY OF DATES

INDEXING BOOKS

———————

BROADCASTING IN BRITAIN (NATIONAL
BOOK LEAGUE)

BIBLIOGRAPHICAL SERVICES THROUGHOUT
THE WORLD, 1950-59 (UNESCO)

LIBRARY ASSISTANCE
TO READERS

by

ROBERT L. COLLISON
Fellow of the Library Association

With a Foreword
by
W. B. STEVENSON
Borough Librarian of Hornsey

PHILOSOPHICAL LIBRARY INC.
15 EAST 40th STREET
NEW YORK 16, N.Y.

© 1963 Crosby Lockwood & Son Ltd, London
Published, 1963 by Philosophical Library, Inc.,
15 East 40th Street, New York 16, N.Y.

_____

Printed in Great Britain for Philosophical Library, Inc., by
Fletcher & Son Ltd, Norwich

Foreword

by W. B. STEVENSON,
Fellow of the Library Association
Borough Librarian of Hornsey

I FIRST wrote an introduction to Mr. Collison's manual when it appeared in 1950; thirteen years later I am glad to introduce this, the fourth revised edition, thoroughly brought up to date. In the intervening years this book has become a standard work on assistance to readers, which is the very heart of librarianship. Here the subject is dealt with in a comprehensive way and the author's contention that this is one of the most satisfying branches of modern work in libraries is more true than ever.

The author emphasizes the importance of good guiding both outside and inside the library. There are still too many public libraries which cannot be distinguished from police stations, banks, and other public buildings, and few librarians have been able to convince their committees that an electric sign outside a library is necessary. Inside the library much progress in guiding and display is evident, and though there is much still to do the interior of the public library of today is much more pleasant and welcoming than it used to be.

This book, however, deals primarily with the technique of tracking down the innumerable enquiries that come from users of the public libraries. The author gives the standard procedure for this work and his maxim that every enquiry should be treated as an important one is very true. The resources of a good library system are now much wider than they were thirteen years ago, and Mr. Collison's added facts and material give a good guide to those resources. The chapter on library service to children and the description of the Sheffield scheme for library training are of the utmost importance; all librarians now realize that the training of future readers should begin in the schools.

The advice given on the duties of a readers' adviser and the systematic compilation of catalogues and booklists should prove of good value, and I welcome the additional sections in this edition on the illustrations collection and the making of indexes. Mr. Collison's ideal of a system which would give, "a definite answer within three days whether any particular book, pamphlet or periodical is available in the United Kingdom" is much nearer possibility in the great development of regional bureaux and national library services. The book is a valuable one, not only to the library student studying for his Library Association examinations, but to all librarians, providing a new look at the essential techniques of the professional library worker.

W. B. STEVENSON

Acknowledgments

THOUGH one name appears on its title-page as author, this book—like many others of all ages—is the outcome of innumerable exchanges of opinion with other people and represents therefore a cross-section of present-day trends. Any good ideas here are thus the property of the library profession as a whole; any bad are due to my errors in transmitting them.

I am especially grateful to Mr J. Bebbington, City Librarian and Information Officer of Sheffield, for providing so many excellent photographs which are reproduced in this edition and which illustrate in detail some of the many aspects of library assistance to readers in a great city. And I am very much indebted to Miss P. E. Charlesworth, Organizer of School Instruction Classes in the Sheffield City Libraries, for revising her very informative chapter on the highly developed service to children for which she is responsible. My thanks are also due to Mr W. B. Stevenson, Borough Librarian of Hornsey, for permission to reprint the forms used in his library, and to the Editor of *The Librarian* for permission to reprint part of the chapter on Directories and Annuals. I am very pleased to have Mr Robert L. Quinsey's guide to the use of catalogues which shows American technique at its best, and to have Dr. William B. Stern's fine photographs of the impressive new Los Angeles County Law Library.

In preparing this edition, I have taken the opportunity not only to revise various matters of fact, but also to eliminate one or two features in order to introduce two new chapters—on Illustrations, and Indexing—to cover aspects of assistance to readers which are rapidly gaining in importance. For the suggestions which prompted these additions, and for the many other letters of comment and criticism, I must thank librarians in many parts of the world.

R. L. C.

Hampstead,
1st January, 1963

TO MY WIFE

Contents

CONTENTS

List of Illustrations and Forms

between pages 62–63

SHEFFIELD CITY LIBRARIES (Plates 1-17)

LOS ANGELES COUNTY LAW LIBRARY

Plates 1-17 are reproduced by courtesy of The Librarian, Sheffield City Libraries and plates 18 and 19 by courtesy of The Librarian, Los Angeles County Law Library.

Forms

Introduction

A PLAN to accompany a guide to the catalogue was commissioned for a new library with a shop front in Central London, and the librarian drew the preliminary sketch on which the students at a nearby art school could base their isometric drawings. When the students visited the library to compare the sketch with the premises for themselves, they pointed out that the librarian's sketch had been drawn from the point of view of the librarian looking *out* of his library towards the street whereas, from the reader's standpoint, it would be far better to base the plan on the reader's first impressions as he entered the library from the street.

This is typical of a natural tendency among librarians—and, indeed, among all specialists—to look at a problem mainly from their own point of view. Owing to periods spent in the Forces many librarians have found themselves in the unexpected position of becoming readers at strange libraries and, in a number of cases for the first time, they have begun to realize the need for much more explicit guiding and assistance to readers than is provided in their own libraries. They have come to realize that while the expert reader with plenty of time to spare for visiting libraries may find the books and information he wants without much difficulty, the average man is usually in a hurry and will neglect to look at any but the plainest of notices. They have begun to recognize the need for repeating announcements since the first notice may very often be missed, and the necessity for offering aid individually wherever possible, since most people will hesitate to approach a desk marked "Enquiries" if the assistant appears to be busy with any type of routine work.

If a customer enters an ironmonger's shop he expects from the assistant behind the counter as much help as is within his power to offer: very often the customer does not know the name of the gadget he needs and can give only a very inadequate description of it. The amount of help he obtains determines his opinion whether the shop is good or bad or just indifferent, and whether he is ever likely to go there again. The same principles of service apply to almost all types of shops and offices. In too many libraries however the staff tend to adopt the attitude (quite unconsciously, it must be admitted) that the reader who already has some knowledge of the ways of the particular library he is using is the most deserving of attention. Thus the reserve stock of a library is tapped mainly by those readers who are accustomed to consulting library catalogues, and its fullest resources will be best exploited by those who have visited it regularly over a long period. Nor, in many cases, do the staff of the average library realize what impression the ordinary reader receives, for the volume of satisfied requests somewhat deadens the impact of any failures, and the number of staff is even now so small that only the most assertive of readers can ensure that he will always receive adequate attention. The man-in-the-street does not like "giving trouble" to people who are obviously working hard, however much he may be encouraged to do so, and it is therefore necessary to give him as much help as possible both directly and indirectly.

Aids to readers to-day go far beyond a handbook or a notice: they include everything which can conceivably help a reader in his choice of a book or in his search for information. The more detailed the assistance given, the more certain will be the satisfaction of the reader. It is not sufficient to present a well-selected stock of books before the eyes of the reader: it is necessary to give him the keys to their best use. That this is essential is due to the enormous growth of even highly-specialized libraries in this century. Whatever the type of library—general or special—the reader is usually confronted with a large amount of reading-matter in which the second-rate is inclined to swamp the more important items. The arrangement of this material may not appear very complicated to the librarian but to the majority of his readers it almost certainly is. In any case the librarian has provided a number of guides—catalogues, classification, etc.—to help his readers to reach every item in the library, but these guides have themselves become so developed in their technique that they themselves need explanatory matter. It is therefore possible in these days of highly-skilled and well-intentioned librarianship for a reader to enter a library and leave it without obtaining the book or information which lies there ready to hand. That this should happen even in a very small minority of cases is something which no librarian would knowingly tolerate. Whatever the cause of such frustration—whether it be a certain degree of obtuseness on the part of the reader, or a lack of appreciating his readers' problems on the part of the librarian—it is something to be eliminated without delay, if the library is to become really efficient, and it is the endeavour of this manual to aid in this purpose.

This book has been written with the point of view of the reader who knows little of libraries or their resources kept well in mind. In a tribunal held some years ago to discuss the dismissal of a librarian is was the chairman's proud boast that he had "never set foot inside a public library!" Had the libraries in the towns he had lived in or visited been more adequately "put on the map", is it not possible that this chairman would have been unable to have made such a singular claim? In preparing publicity librarians are often apt to assume that certain facts about their libraries are so well known and so obvious that they are not worth repeating. Even if they are known to all the present readers or potential readers—and this is certainly improbable—each year a new generation grows up which knows little of what services are available. In addition, the movement of population is still increasing: every train and bus brings strangers to the town who do not know even the name of the main street or the early-closing day, much less what libraries there are or where they are situated. The technique of keeping the public informed and of assisting people has been highly developed by other public services which leave the stranger in no doubt as to what street he is in or where he may cross it, and the librarian will see from their methods that no basic knowledge on the part of the public

xvii

is assumed, all information being repeated and couched in the simplest unambiguous terms.

It has not proved possible to treat in detail the problems of the advanced worker and the highly specialized library. Those who have read the late Dr S. C. Bradford's book on *Documentation* (2nd edition, with an Introduction by Dr Jesse H. Shera and Professor Margaret E. Egan, London, Crosby Lockwood, 1953)* will remember his description of the needs of the scientist and of the difficulties encountered by scientific and technical libraries. The type of services he there proposes are all an extension of the work of helping readers but are best read and considered in Dr Bradford's own words.

* New edition in preparation.

Part I

THE LIBRARY

External and General Notices and Signs

THE great majority of libraries are well concealed from public notice. In the nineteenth-century when many of the libraries of present-day importance were built, it was generally accepted that a library should be placed *near* but not *in* a well-frequented part. They were further hindered by a florid and wasteful form of architecture which current taste finds somewhat distasteful and is therefore inclined to ignore. The combination of elaborate design with last-minute economies in interior decoration and furnishings has left subsequent generations with costly and inefficient buildings which are unworthy of their task. Much has been done to remedy this in recent years: the newer buildings which have been erected have often been well designed and strategically located: nevertheless, in common with their predecessors, they sometimes present long stretches of wall and window without any form of display or notice beyond an official announcement or a foundation stone. It was thus possible for several third-year students in a large American university to confess recently that they had never made use of their university library (which is very well stocked and admirably administered), just as in many a provincial town in Britain the local resident is unable to give a stranger precise information concerning the position of the nearest public library.

The concealment of libraries in this fashion has rarely achieved its purpose: back streets and cul-de-sacs are notoriously considered the most convenient for the loading of trucks, the parking of vehicles, and therefore the best sites for traffic jams. It is in these places in fact that the lives of the public are most endangered. Nor has the modern practice of setting a library well back from the thoroughfare behind banks of flowering-plants and carefully-tended lawns much to recommend it beyond an aesthetic satisfaction, for the public will pass such a building daily without bothering to find out what purpose it serves. It has yet to be established that a library is a public service which needs to be sited in a position which the public can reach without making wide detours from their usual itinerary, and without exposing themselves unduly to the inclemencies of the weather. Every business man knows that the siting of any kind of premises even slightly off the main stream of traffic (or on the wrong side of the road) will prevent the busy housewife or the hurried worker from using them except when absolutely driven by necessity to do so. Public authorities still remain to be convinced that the same principle applies to the libraries under their control.

Whatever the position of the library, it is essential that it should be made widely known. Permission should be obtained to erect notices on lamp-posts and street corners directing people to the library. It is not sufficient to do so without making provision for their maintenance in good condition: in many places old, misleading and half-obliterated notices are to be seen: their neglect produces a very bad impression and will not encourage people to visit the library. All notices should be planned to start from the busiest areas and be repeated at the intersection of any two roads where there is any danger of the reader mistaking his route.

In addition, it should be ensured that the position of the library is plainly marked on all maps and guides issued for the use of the public whether officially or unofficially. A check on local maps will sometimes reveal that the position of public buildings is sufficiently ambiguously shown that strangers to the district might easily miss the library altogether on a dark night or at any time when they are in a hurry. Only the utmost vigilance can ensure that the library is correctly sited and named. And, if the library is situate at some distance from other public buildings, it is well to make certain that their doorkeepers and "Enquiries" assistants are able to give correct instructions on how to reach it.

Once the reader has reached the correct thoroughfare he should never be in a position to wonder which is the building housing the library. Public buildings do not usually use a street number: in a long street this may be a cause of considerable embarrassment to the new reader. Signs at both ends of the street should direct the reader and the building itself should be plainly marked—there should be no possibility for the reader's mistaking it for any of the buildings which official architecture makes it resemble—police stations, laboratories, clubs, or telephone exchanges. A library can be adequately marked—without appearing unsightly—by a projecting sign placed high enough to be seen over the heads of passers-by, but low enough to be seen from a car, and this sign should be illuminated at night. It should be so designed that it can be read from either side, and large enough to be plainly visible across the street—and it should be kept in good repair.

Some readers of this book may feel that so much guidance is unnecessary, but those who have had any experience of directing the public to such buildings as Olympia or Carnegie Hall from quite near by will realize that guidance cannot be too detailed or repeated overmuch.

Buildings and Departments

ONE of the most frequent causes of disappointment to readers is their arrival at the library at a time when it is closed. The hours of opening should be printed in all guide books and directories, included on all public notices (including, if possible, all street signs directing to the library), printed in all the library's publications, and exhibited plainly on the street frontage of the library. Thus, if the library lies behind ornamental gardens it should be possible for the public to know whether the library is open or not without having to cross a large open space in bad weather. In any case it should be possible for the public to know the hours of opening without actually entering the building. And the hours of opening should be printed on all correspondence, especially reserve and overdue notices.

Any notice placed outside a library which gives the hours of opening should also enumerate the departments available to the public. It has been known for readers to penetrate as far as the caretaker's flat in search of a non-existent newsroom. In the same way, any alteration of times due to public holidays, redecoration or structural repairs, etc., should be plainly exhibited well in advance of the period affected and outside the building as well as inside. Members of the public should be left in no doubt concerning what facilities are available to them at any hour of any particular day.

A wide-mouthed letter-box with self-closing flap should be placed near the entrance for the return of books at times when the library is closed. This feature is looked upon with disfavour by some librarians who feel that it can be used for avoiding the payment of fines. Against this however must be set the overwhelming advantage of the convenience of those members of the public who arrive too late to hand in their books in the ordinary way. After all, the return of the books themselves is what the librarian principally desires, and the question of the settlement of any outstanding fines can be made dependent on the return of the reader's tickets and permission to borrow further books. Such a letter-box should be clearly marked RETURNED BOOKS and should be illuminated in the evening.

On entering the building the reader should immediately find clear guides directing him to whatever part of the library he wishes to visit. Ideally an Enquiries Desk is desirable, but few libraries have space or sufficient staff to spare for this, and its place must be taken by signs directing the readers to the various departments of the library. Here again any signs directing the readers to departments on other floors should give the hours of opening if they vary from those given at the entrance to avoid wasting the public's time. The separation of departments should be especially noted: thus the divorce of directories and yearbooks from the main Reference Library, or the Adolescent Collection from the Children's Department, should be made known.

All doors and entrances should be marked: if public, with the name of the department: if for staff use only, with the word PRIVATE. Any staircases not intended for public use should be roped off and also marked private. In short, it should not be possible for any reader to mistake one department for another, to be unaware of the existence of any facility, or to enter any part of the building not designed for his use.

Just inside the entrance to the library should be placed a well-illuminated plan of the entire building, showing the position of the departments in relation to each other. In making such a plan it is useful to use an isometric or similar projection which will give a three-dimensional impression and thus improve its chances of being understood by the readers.

All signs and plans should be so designed that they bear useful information on both front and back if they project from the wall, hang from the ceiling, or are fixed on island stands. They should be clearly worded in letters capable of being easily read from a distance of ten or twelve feet, and should be placed at a height sufficient to allow of their being read over the shoulders of intervening readers. Particular care should be maintained at all times to ensure that no notice is left up once it is out-of-date or has served its purpose.

If the library has branches in outlying areas, or a travelling library service, full details—including addresses, hours of opening and telephone numbers—should be displayed, preferably where readers can see them as they leave the library. Similarly notices of extension activities—lectures, concerts, etc.,—are best displayed facing the entrances to departments, since readers are more likely to look at them when they are leaving rather than in their hurry to enter a department.

The Lending Library

AS the reader enters the lending library he should be left in no doubt as to which side of the counter or desk he should go to return his books. If possible the "blind" side of the counter facing the entrance, which is often protected from draughts by a glass screen, should be provided with an Enquiries guichet for the use of new readers.

The lay-out of the average lending library, especially if it has many island or alcove stacks, is confusing to the reader. It is not easy for him to grasp the lay-out as a whole or to get any clearer impression than that of a large collection of books housed in a crowded mass around narrow aisles. His impression is even less clear when there are many readers in the library and where there is much movement of public and staff. To help him it is essential to provide a number of aids, the first of which is a good plan of the department. The plan should again be on the isometric principle and should be based on the entrance, showing clearly the position of the bookstacks and the catalogue in relation to the desk or counter. The main contents of each stack should be marked on the plan, and the position of adjacent departments—if they can be reached from the lending library—should also be shown.

Several copies of this plan should be made. One should be inset under a glass cover on the "in" side of the counter where readers can study it during slack periods—while their books are being discharged. Others should be placed near the catalogues and at strategic positions throughout the department where readers may have a chance to study them. Thus, if tables and chairs are provided for readers, it would be well to inset a copy of the plan on each table top. The blind ends of bookstacks are also good places for plans, provided that there is sufficient space in front of them for readers to stand and study the plan without impeding others. Each copy of the plan should invite the readers to ask the staff for further information.

There are many people to whom the study of plans does not appeal: for these, and further to assist all readers, the bookstacks and their contents must be individually guided. Each bookstack should have its main contents indicated: in addition, the contents of each tier should be displayed directly above it in smaller lettering. The blind ends of bookstacks should also have their main contents shown. The methods of indicating the contents of bookstacks are many: some libraries hang framed printed or hand-lettered signs on the stacks, others have them lettered directly on to the wood or metal stack itself. Some of the older libraries with tall bookstacks have filled in the top shelves with notices of

the contents of the tiers. A few hang the signs like banners projecting from either end of each stack, while some of the more-
recently erected libraries use removable coloured plastic letters
which often look very effective and can be read easily from a
distance. A visit to a well-planned modern bookshop will provide additional ideas, just as the study of any large department
store will prove a useful lesson in adequate methods of guiding
the public well and unobtrusively. The method which is most
suited to the needs of the individual library should be chosen, and
the wording of the notices should be carefully chosen to suit the
readers for whom it is intended. Thus the word LANGUAGES
is more likely to awaken interest than the term PHILOLOGY
in a general library.

It is not sufficient to guide the bookstacks and the tiers: in
many cases the shelves themselves should also have some indication of their contents. It was once the practice to fix one or more
subject guides to each shelf: later there was a natural reaction
which tended toward the removal of all shelf guides. The more
sensible method is to make a shelf guide wherever there is an
important subject on which the library has a representative
collection of material. Thus even the smallest general library has
a shelf or more of medical books, and medicine is a subject for
which most readers look from time to time: this is a clear case for
a shelf guide.

Shelf guides are of many types: some are lettered on blocks or
metal brackets shelved between the books, while others are small
slips held in metal containers on the outer edge of the shelf. Still
others are attached to the uprights supporting the shelves, and
some libraries have even lettered the contents directly on to the
outer edges of the shelves (a practice to be avoided as it prevents
the free interchange of shelves and the movement of classes of
books). Here again the choice must be suited to the library's
particular needs: the main features to be desired in all notices
are that they should be effective without being unduly obtrusive.
The reader is unaware of effective guidance: he makes use of it
without being conscious of its existence. It is only its absence or

inadequacy which stirs him to criticism. As a general rule it should be assumed that where movement of stock is rapid—as in a small library with large issues—it is best to employ movable guides of a type which can easily and swiftly be fitted in a new position. In such libraries elaborate lettering direct on to the stacks and shelves themselves is wasteful and misleading: its practice should be kept for more static material where extensive change is unlikely.

Not only the library and its departments, the bookstacks, tiers and shelves should be guided, but also each individual book by means of its classification number, since this is really a shorthand version of its subject. The classification number should be clearly lettered on the lower portion of the spine of the book: if it is a long number the first three figures should be lettered boldly and the rest in smaller figures, thus:—

$$\textbf{621}$$
$$\textbf{384}$$

and it should also be ensured that the title on the spine of the book corresponds with that on the title-page and in the catalogue. If there is any discrepancy the title on the spine should be altered sufficiently to ensure identification. Examples of this are the omission of the title or of the author's name, or the printing of the publisher's name alone in the case of trade publications. Where the book is too slim to bear a title or number on its spine, the author's surname, brief title, and classification number should be lettered on the top left-hand corner of the front cover, since this often projects above neighbouring books and, in any case is most clearly seen as soon as the volume is drawn out from its fellows.

Where, owing to the smallness of the department or the size of the stock, there is a large reserve of material which is not visible to the public, it is to their advantage to remind readers of this fact—particularly at those shelves where this message particularly applies. Thus most general libraries have large collections of books on the locality in which they are situate: if there is not room on the shelves to display more than a fraction of the material, a notice to this effect on the actual shelf containing books of local interest will help to overcome this difficulty. It is true that such resources are fully revealed by the catalogue, but many readers never make use of catalogues and assume that what they see is all that is available.

The Reference Library

THE guiding of the reference library is a more satisfactory business from the point of view of both librarian and reader. In the first place, unlike the stock of the lending library, the reference stock is rarely removed long from the shelves and thus a shelf guide is usually left with sufficient books to support its statement of what the shelf contains. Furthermore, the reference department is not used to the same extent as a modern lending library, and there is usually more opportunity to move round the shelves in an unhurried fashion and to study their contents at leisure, being sure too that the important as well as the supporting material on a subject is to be found there. Again, it is often possible to see the lay-out of a reference library as a whole since it is rarely impeded with island bookstacks.

As the reader enters the reference library, a plan of the department should be the first thing to meet his gaze. If the assistant's desk is placed conveniently near, the reader will then be assured of an adequate introduction to the department. Bookstacks, tiers and shelves should all be clearly marked with their contents and, since there is more opportunity to study these notices, they can be worded rather more fully.

The problems of a reference library are somewhat more complicated than those of a lending department in some respects. For instance, like an iceberg, many a reference library can only show to the readers a small proportion of its total resources. The reserve stock of a reference library contains many large sets of books, and some libraries attempt to indicate their presence by placing the first (and sometimes the index) volume of each set on the public shelves, with a notice pasted inside to the effect that the rest of the volumes "can be consulted on application". In theory this method could not be bettered: its is surprising, however, in practice, how few times readers will avail themselves of this opportunity. Again, many types of reference material—maps, pamphlets, illustrations, microfilms, etc.—are not suitable for display on open shelves, so that their exploitation must be left to the members of the staff and to adequate cataloguing and indexing.

Another problem is that of the very varying size of reference books. Nearly every reference library has at least three sequences of books—octavo, quarto and folio—and some have a fourth for elephant folios. This system enables the utmost economy in shelf space to be secured, and helps the staff to find books easily and quickly, but it is a drawback for the reader since (1) the parallel sequences rarely bring books on the same subject near each other, and (2) the reader is often unaware of the existence of other books on the same subject owing to their being shelved in a separate sequence. Here again the reader is dependent on the staff and the catalogue for ensuring that he gains access to the full resources of the library.

Owing to theft and mis-use it is the practice in many reference libraries to remove popular and important works from the main sequence and shelve them in the staff enclosure or in some part not open to the public. There is no objection to this method providing that the availability of such books is shown by notices plainly displayed at the points on the shelves at which they would normally appear.

In addition, some reference libraries have special facilities available, such as large collections on special subjects housed separately, carrels for private study, or copying services. These facilities should all be made known to readers and not be left to be discovered during some chance conversation with a member of the staff. One such service which is offered by many libraries and even now is insufficiently exploited is the availability of considerable back files of newspapers, periodicals and the proceedings of learned societies, and yet in these is contained the first news of important advances of knowledge which can ill afford to be ignored.

It is not sufficient for the experienced reader at a library to know what resources he may reasonably expect to find in the reference department: the same information should be given to every chance visitor to the library, no matter what department he uses. When an eminent librarian spoke on the radio in the Woman's Hour, he mentioned three simple services such as every reference library offers as a matter of course. For days afterwards he received numbers of appreciative letters from intelligent listeners, the burden of which was "I never knew such useful services were available locally". It is obvious that libraries have yet far to go in making known their everyday services to their readers.

Public Information Bureaux

PUBLIC information bureaux are sometimes housed in the local public library: more often they are placed strategically at busy points in the town where the greatest number of people are likely to notice them, but even so they are often administered by the public library of the area. Whether they are administered separately or as part of the local library services, their interests have much in common with the latter and careful planning is necessary if unnecessary duplication of work is to be avoided. The best way to achieve this is to define the work of such bureaux which have functions which the ordinary reference department only partly attempts to perform.

The most usual types of public information bureaux are those concerned with civic information and with holidays. The civic information bureau attempts to advise people on problems affecting their everyday life: such subjects as housing, medical supplies and facilities, family troubles, problems with regard to insurance or pensions, etc., are typical of their daily routine. The answers to such difficulties are to be found only partly in books and printed matter: while a collection of this material is a necessary part of the bureau, it would in itself be insufficient to carry out this work. What is needed, in addition, is staff experienced in the handling of these problems and who have personal knowledge of temporary legislation, regulations, local and national welfare services, and the functions of the appropriate local and national government departments in relation to members of the public who are in difficulty. It has been proved that library staffs are capable of performing this work very successfully, but to do so they need special training.

The function of a library is to provide information from published sources: the civic information bureau adds to this by providing information based on experience of similar cases in the past, by putting the public in touch with experts and with official departments, and by seeing to it that welfare services and charitable organizations are contacted wherever there is a definite need for their help. There is thus a case at all times for the closest collaboration between the library and the civic information bureau and, where the latter is not provided independently, there is a strong argument for its being set up under public library auspices as part of the normal service to readers.

Holiday information bureaux have come to be an accepted feature of many towns on which the public increasingly relies for the successful planning of its holidays. The provision of guides to holiday resorts is not sufficient: this is only the basic material and it must be supported by much other material. Standard guide books, topographical works, maps—Ordnance Survey, road, rail, hikers, waterways, ancient monuments, historical sites, mountaineering, etc.—timetables (air, rail, bus, coach, steamer, etc.), details of domestic and foreign tours, youth hostel and camping and cycling and hiking guides, hotel, farm and boarding house directories, and similar material are all essential features of the stock-in-trade of the efficient holiday information bureau. Nor must cheap holidays—including holidays at home, local events, half-day trips and excursions, etc.—be ignored. Moreover, close co-operation must be built up with local travel and tourist agencies, and with the national associations connected with travel and holidays.

Other Departments

THE guiding of other departments of the library is based on the same principles governing that of lending and reference libraries. All effective guiding is largely a matter of common-sense, coupled with an ability to see the library from the reader's point of view: yet ridiculous, ambiguous and misleading notices continue to be displayed from time to time owing to lack of foresight.

The department usually most neglected by the framers of notices is the newspaper and periodical room. In many libraries this, the most used, is also the Cinderella of all departments, and is treated as such by staff and public alike. There is no necessity for such an attitude: most people get great delight from reading their favourite periodicals and only assume an appearance of mute misery when obliged to read them in an institutional-like atmosphere surrounded by notices of SILENCE and DO NOT SPIT. Near the entrance to the Department a list of newspapers and periodicals available should be displayed—and the avail-ability of files of back issues should be made known. This list should be in alphabetical order of titles, and there should be an additional list in subject order for the convenience of the great majority of readers who are not familiar with every item which is published on the subjects in which they are interested. Addi-tional copies of the lists should be placed on the periodicals rack and on each of the walls of the room. Ideally, a trained assistant (armed with copies of *Willing's*, the *Newspaper press directory*, *Gregory*, *Ayer's*, *Ulrich*, the *World list*, and the *British union catalogue of periodicals*), should be stationed in this room ready to answer enquiries and to supply back numbers of periodicals. In addition, there should be indexes to the contents of the periodicals (*see* page 119). If this is not possible, notices should be displayed saying that such facilities are available in the reference library. The periodical covers, if they are filed in order of number, should be plainly marked on their spines with both title and number, and they should have the type of "window" or transparent cover which will enable them to be recognized however they lie on the tables. And if there is any discrepancy between the published date of the periodical and the date it actually arrives (as in the case of foreign periodicals and the publications of some learned societies) a notice to this effect should be affixed to the cover.

Reader's guidance in the children's library is a subject on its own which requires special consideration and treatment. Suffice it to say that all notices should be worded to suit the level of understanding of their readers, and that shelf and tier guiding should be simple and bold, while illustrations will add to the effectiveness of words, and a model rather than a plan of the department will be far more successful in explaining to children the arrangement of the contents of their library.

Most public libraries have a collection of local material, and it is rare that its resources are fully exploited by the many members of the public who might reasonably be expected to be interested in it. This is partly the fault of inadequate guiding. Consider the contents of an average local collection: it includes the history, topography and antiquities of the area; works on the genealogy and history of local families; ecclesiastical surveys and history; local directories; biographies of local worthies; works by local authors, and sometimes books locally printed and published; prints, paintings, drawings, portraits, maps, plans, posters, notices, playbills, programmes, tradesmen's cards, etc.—all of local interest. Then there is the archive material: charters, deeds, rate books, manorial and other court records, poll books, documents relating to local societies and institutions, families, and local business firms. Much of this material is not suited to any kind of display. Here the exploitation must be based on close classification, careful analytical cataloguing, good printed guides, and frequently-changed effective displays of local material of particular or topical interest. And in this connection, the presence of a member of the staff with a real interest in and knowledge of the subject is the best adjunct to such a collection.

Among other departments sometimes provided are a business or a commercial and technical library whose users are mostly in a hurry: here notices need to be brief and bold—DIRECTORIES, PATENTS, ANNUALS, and so on. Everything in such a department must be designed from the point of view of the man standing hesitantly at the entrance and gazing round the shelves: from his position he should be able to read every important sign and should also be able to study a good plan of the department. An Enquiries Desk should be facing or at one side of the door.

Intermediate libraries for adolescents can safely demand a fairly high degree of comprehension and intelligence on the part of the reader. The adolescent reader is intellectually alive, his faculties have been sharpened by the competition and interests of school life, and he is habituated to the effort necessary to understand new things. He may safely be required to read straightforward explanations of the classification and the use of catalogues, to grasp a clear plan of the department and to and his way about the shelves with a moderate amount of help.

The problems of music and gramophone record collections are too specialized to be treated here: the principles are however fundamentally the same and only require adaptation to the types of material being handled.*

Displays

IN every library there is sufficient material for an endless series of displays of books and material on subjects of both general and sectional interest. Unlike a bookshop, whose potential influence is often somewhat impeded by commercial considerations, the library can give prominence to cultural interests of even limited appeal; at the same time it can also devote other displays to more popular tastes. There should be no excuse for the assistant

* See the United Kingdom Branch of the International Association of Music Libraries' *Gramophone Record Libraries* (Crosby Lockwood, 1963).

who neglects to change a display on the plea that he can think of no new subject, all the obvious ones having already been used. If this is really so, there is no reason why a subject previously used should not be revived under a new title—journalists annually revive the well-worn subjects of Spring, the Easter egg and Christmas without any visible drop in interest on the part of the public. But a glance at the day's news will usually provide sufficient inspiration for more than one new display, and rejected ideas should be noted for reconsideration for possible future use.

The purpose of displays should not be solely the exploitation of neglected stock: the interests of the readers must come first. Fortunately these two aims often coincide or at least overlap to a certain extent; where they do not, the display itself is usually ignored.

Displays are endless in their variety: they may roughly be divided into the following categories:

(a) topical—anniversaries, outstanding events, etc.;
(b) subject—bringing together books on the same or related subjects which, by reason of classification or size, may ordinarily be separated on the shelves;
(c) individual author—bringing together the works of an author who has written on a wide variety of subjects;
(d) new books—to keep the public in touch with what has recently been added to the library;
(e) exhibitions—displays of books in connection with events in, or outside the library: book weeks, local lectures, etc.

Under section (a) would be included displays in connection with broadcasts taking place the same day or in the near future. The subject displays under (b) would help to exploit the reserve stock not ordinarily visible to readers and thus show that much more is available on request. Section (c) would help to bring to the reader's notice works by authors in which he is interested and which he might otherwise have missed.

Displays should not be restricted to one form of material or one department: they should cover the full resources of the library and should include periodicals, paintings and drawings, maps, plans, prints, and any other non-book material wherever it is appropriate. In the same way, whatever the department in which the display is actually put, material from other departments should always be included wherever it has a definite bearing on the subject illustrated.

The display of book-jackets is still one of the most popular forms of publicizing recent additions to a library, but its popularity is mainly restricted to the members of the staff since, unless the books themselves are actually available when asked for, the readers find such displays more irritating than helpful. Dust-jackets, being designed to sell the books, are decorative, effective and readily lend themselves to attractive arrangement. It is suggested however that they should be changed as soon as the books they represent have been issued, unless it is reasonably certain that other copies will be available within a few days to meet the demand their display has created.

Displays need not be restricted to the library itself: they can be placed on the street front where they will attract new readers, or they can be placed at vantage points elsewhere in the town. Some libraries make use of the windows of the showrooms of local public utilities, or fix a glass-case or display-board in the main entrance hall of the town hall, or even borrow space in the show-windows of the local department-store. The possibilities are endless providing the displays are frequently changed and do not lose their interest. A study of the methods of experienced advertisers will show in this connection that very frequent change is usually necessary, and even a short time spent watching the public's reaction to displays in shop windows will demonstrate that a high standard of arrangement, lighting, etc., is necessary to attract the attention of the somewhat sophisticated tastes of to-day.

In the library itself displays of books are very often difficult to organize effectively since the stock of a busy library soon loses its new appearance and its exploitation must rely mainly on notices with a strong appeal. It is possible to utilize a certain number of permanent one-book displays for small spaces—such as the blind ends of bookstacks—with titles such as IN THE NEWS, BOOK OF TO-DAY, TO-DAY'S CLASSIC, ON THE AIR, TV CHOICE, etc. This allows for the emphasis of subjects represented in the library's stock by only a few books, and also facilitates the quick exploitation of news since no new notice has to be prepared before a book can be displayed. There is also the point that many readers, who are unattracted by the larger displays, will at least pause to glance at a book which is considered sufficiently important to be displayed on its own.

Small troughs, holding twelve to twenty books, designed either as table models (they are sometimes built into the table) or on stands, are well suited to library purposes. Surmounted by simple notices they draw constant attention and, if their contents are well chosen and the subject topical or popular, the books will not long remain in the trough and will need frequent replacement. Where special furniture is not available or where there is no space for special fittings, it is possible to use isolated shelves (even in the middle of the fiction shelves) to display a handful of books supported by a notice which either stands on the shelf or covers part of the shelves, or to clear a complete tier and prepare a more elaborate display supported by large posters, models, etc. Illustrative material—fishing tackle for an exhibit on fishing, gadgets for a display on "how to do it yourself", etc.—can quite often be borrowed from nearby shops providing acknowledgment is made of the source of the objects: where costly items are used they can be covered by short-term insurance. If this kind of display can be done well it is worth doing: if not, and if the results would appear amateurish, it is best left alone.

If displays are to be effective they need constant attention: no extraneous book should be allowed to stray into them for very long, and no display should become even temporarily empty—this implies that there should always be on hand a small reserve of suitable material ready to replace what has been taken by readers. There is one point that is worth special attention: some members of the public will hesitate to take books from a display, believing that the volumes are put there for inspection only. This mis-apprehension should be removed by fixing a small permanent notice to all display fittings saying that readers are welcome to take any book shown there.

One of the most popular of all displays if done well is that exhibiting books "recommended by the staff". This is under-standable, for there are many more readers who would like the help of the staff than those who actually ask for it. One of the great points of appeal of such a display is its miscellaneous nature: like dipping into a bran tub, the reader is never certain what he is likely to get, but he feels that he has the chance of dis-covering something very good. For such a display to be perman-ently successful, however, it is essential that the staff—and every one of them should contribute to it frequently—should only put in it what has proved of exceptional interest to them-selves. Thus, instead of making it a vehicle for the pushing of minor and neglected classics, etc., they should put on it the light-est as well as the most serious, the newest as well as the rather aged, of the stock in their library—the only qualification should be that whatever volume is put there is capable of being defended by at least one member of the staff as something worth attention.

A special feature of some libraries is the wholesale removal of favourite types of books such as romances, wild west stories, detective and thriller tales, from the main sequence and shelving them separately at convenient points. This policy is vehemently opposed by many librarians who consider that it is pandering to the lowest tastes of the public. Be that as it may, the sorting-out of popular forms of books is a definite service to the busy reader who has only ten minutes or so between buses or on the way to work in which to choose a book. The main point, if such a system is adopted, is to see that only such books as fit the genre are displayed, and that displays of this kind are not used as means of palming off unpopular works. The reader who finds that by using a display he has chosen a book which does not suit his tastes will naturally be wary of trusting to it a second time.

It is sometimes possible to stimulate or revive interest in a subject by somewhat elaborate displays of material other than books. Thus, the display of a model of the new town planning scheme relating to the locality will undoubtedly awaken interest in books and periodicals on town planning if a good selection of works on that subject is exhibited close by; an exhibition of local antiquities may well stimulate interest in local history. Such displays, to promote a more permanent interest, are best supported by the issue of booklists, catalogues, or bibliographies on the subject, and their preparation and production will be discussed later.

The introduction of displays should not lightly be attempted: once undertaken, displays should be maintained efficiently, regularly and effectively. No pains should be spared to keep them alive in their approach and of a high standard in their production; good lettering is of course of the greatest importance. Wherever there is a choice of books which can be shown, those which have the best printing and format should always be selected. Poor work and bad book-selection should not be tolerated: too many libraries have displays which languish in their appeal owing to insufficient planning and subsequent neglect.

Guide to the Classification

WHATEVER form of classification is used in the library, it needs a number of guides to its use if the reader is to gain the full benefit from its system. Although a good library classification is logical and planned to suit the reader's requirements, it is by no means self-explanatory and, unless the reader is acquainted with the principles on which it is constructed, he is likely to overlook books which may be of great interest to him. Thus the student of agriculture, who is a member of a library classified by the Dewey Decimal Classification, may make use of the technical volumes in the 630 section for a considerable time without realizing that the economic aspects of his subject are shelved at 338.

In the handbook to the library (whose production and contents are discussed on page 32), a chapter should certainly be devoted to the classification scheme and its use. In addition, the plan of the library should include not only the names of the main subjects but also their classification numbers. The lettering or notices above the bookcases should include the classification numbers and so should the individual tier and shelf guides.

The Readers' Adviser (see page 54) should have a complete copy of the classification scheme, and two or three copies of the index to the classification should be displayed prominently where the readers will make use of them. Where the catalogue in use has a classified subject section, there will also be the additional aid of an index to the subjects represented by entries in that catalogue. In addition, shorter alphabetical lists of the hundred or five hundred or one thousand most popular subjects (based on recent issues of books to readers) should be prepared in pamphlet form for distribution on a liberal scale to readers.

When new readers join the library, the Readers' Adviser should furnish them with a list of the relevant classification numbers for subjects in which they are most interested: it is noticeable that nowadays many readers memorize the Dewey classification numbers of their own subjects and look for them in every library they visit. Whenever booklists, library bulletins, bibliographies or any other form of publicity are issued, all books mentioned should be accompanied by their classification numbers. In addition, any popular introductions to public libraries should be included liberally in the lending and reference stock.

In spite of this, many readers will remain entirely dependent on the staff for aid and they must be encouraged by invitations in notice form to ask the staff for help at all times. In the children's and intermediate or adolescent departments it is possible to educate the new generations as they grow up by means of lectures, competitions, practical library work—especially shelving and putting books in order—and handbooks (see pages 87 and 94), so that in the near future we may look forward to a well-informed public expecting and capable of making good use of a high standard of classification in the libraries which it uses.

Guides to the Catalogues

THE modern library catalogue, whatever its form—card, sheaf or printed book—especially in the larger libraries, is a formidable affair in appearance and would certainly, by itself, be rarely used.

Its use needs considerable explanation in a brief and palatable form, and also the assistance of the Readers' Adviser wherever possible. A chapter of the handbook to the library (see page 32) should be devoted to its explanation, and any general works on libraries which include explanations of the use of catalogues should be added to the stock of all adult departments.

Each catalogue should be surmounted by a short guide to its use, and should include the following items:

(i) explanation of the method of identifying a book by its author, subject or title,

(ii) explanation of the main rules of alphabetization in use in that particular library (unfortunately the rules of alphabetization still vary very much even within individual countries, so that it is possible for a reader who is used to one system to miss items when making use of a catalogue or index constructed under a different set of rules),

(iii) explanation of the method of finding a book on the shelves.

The guide should also be reprinted in pamphlet form and distributed as liberally as possible, or at least to all new members. In addition, lectures on the use of the catalogues should be given in schools and in the children's and intermediate or adolescent departments (see pages 87 and 94), classes from local schools should be encouraged to make occasional visits to the reference library to practise finding books with the aid of the catalogues and the classification, and competitions and practical work with the catalogues should be a regular feature of routine in the departments serving children and adolescents.

The contents of the catalogue drawers or the sheaf holders

should be well guided both within and without. Each drawer or sheaf holder should be clearly labelled with its contents, for example:

| BOR—BOX | ALLEN—ARMOR | 629—629.2 |

and the contents should be fully guided with class and sub-division guides showing the ramifications of each subject and groups of subjects at a glance, and giving references to related subjects in other parts of the classification scheme. Symbols, however, are not understood by the great majority of children, and the guide should therefore be by name:

| BLYTON—BORROW |

It is a good plan to introduce new readers to the sections in the catalogue containing entries on the subjects in which they are interested, and to advise them to inspect these sections regularly for new additions. This procedure can be included in the Readers' Adviser's general introduction to the library (see page 55). Such readers will often follow up references to other subjects if they find that the catalogue repays careful study.

Many of the university libraries in the United States issue each year a printed guide for the use of newcomers. One of the liveliest of these is *Students and libraries* which is published by the University of Kansas. The latest edition, obtainable from the Director of Libraries, University of Kansas, Lawrence, Kansas, includes the following guide to the catalogues; it is supported by diagrams of printed catalogue cards, in which such items as call number, author, title, etc., are indicated by red pointers.

THE CARD CATALOG

The main Card Catalog is a long series of alphabetized cards which constitutes in a broad sense a detailed index to the Library's holdings. For practically every book in the Library, there is at least one card in the Catalog, and usually there are several. The *main card* is filed under the author's last name. In some cases, the author of a book may nominally be an institution (American Museum of Natural History), a branch of a government (U.S. Geological Survey), or some other impersonal agency.

Ordinarily there is also in the Catalog at least one *subject card* for a given book, filed under the appropriate descriptive subject of the book's contents; sometimes there are several such cards. The subject is typed in red at the top of the card.

A third kind of catalog card for a given book is a *title card*, which is usually made only for distinctive titles. For example, you may expect to find a title card for *The folklore of capitalism* but not for *A textbook of modern economics*.

The Card Catalog will therefore provide the answers to these questions:·

(1)   What books does the Library have by a particular author?
(2)   What books does the Library have relating to a particular subject?
(3)   Does the Library have a book with a particular title?

The cards in the catalog provide a great deal of additional information: the call number, the author's full name, and the text of the title page, followed by the place of publication, name of publisher, date, and often such other data as the number of pages, notes of illustrations, bibliographies.

Learning a few of the catalog filing practices will greatly facilitate your searches for materials. For example, names beginning with *Mac*, *Mc*, or *M'*, are filed as though spelled *Mac*. Numerals are filed as though spelled out in full. All filing disregards initial articles, *A*, *An*, and *The*, in any language.

Part II

PUBLICATIONS

Aids to the Readers' Adviser

THERE are a number of indispensable reference works which the Readers' Adviser needs at all times. The different departments of the library have conflicting claims on most of them, but if the Readers' Adviser is not to be hampered in his work, it is essential that they should be by his desk. If, every time the Readers' Adviser has to consult a standard reference book, he has to refer to the Reference Library or to the Cataloguing Department, much time is wasted and there will be a certain natural hesitation in calling too much on the help of other staff. The more bibliographies, both general and specialized, which the Adviser has immediately available, the more efficient his work will be.

The Readers' Adviser should be able to answer any question concerning the published material in the English language issued during the last ten years. This entails his having a complete set of the *British National Bibliography*, and ten-year files and current issues of both Whitaker's *Cumulative Book List* and the H. W. Wilson Company's *Cumulative Book Index*—including the cumulative volumes of each. The *Cumulative Book Index* is essential since it is especially thorough in indexing American and British Commonwealth publications not only by author and title but also by subject, the single sequence of entries enabling books to be identified without delay.

Many requests concern non-commercial publications, especially those issued by government departments, public corporations and international agencies. The Adviser should be provided with a ten-year file and current monthly issues of the catalogues of H.M.S.O., and should also have indexes to the publications of the U.S. Government and to the documents issued by the United Nations Organization and its agencies if the work of the individual library warrants their provision.

In addition to these the Adviser should have at hand the

catalogues of the chief British and American publishers, a current list of technical publications—such as the *ASLIB Book List* or *Technical Book Review*—Cotton and Glencross's *Fiction Index*, Baker's *Best Fiction* and *Historical Fiction*, the H. W. Wilson Company's *Fiction Catalog*, the latest edition of Hoffman's *Reader's Adviser and Bookman's Manual*, Keller's *Reader's Digest*, the British Drama League's *Player's Library* and its supplements, Gardner's *Sequels*, French's *Guide to Plays*, the series of literary biographical dictionaries by Kunitz and Haycraft, and the recent additions lists of the more important government libraries and of the libraries of such institutions as the London School of Economics, the Royal Institute of British Architects, etc., and the annual accessions lists of the University of London library.

If possible, the later volumes of the subject index of the British Museum should be provided: many enquiries are made concerning what has been published on specific subjects, and the British Museum subject index is especially helpful since it lists the outstanding foreign publications as well as those in the English language. In this connection, the subject indexes issued by the London Library are of the greatest help in dealing with enquiries on non-technical subjects. An additional tool of increasing value is the annual American *Subject Guide to Books in Print* which includes a remarkable amount of British books and which is superbly arranged and cross-referenced.

Sonnenschein's *Best Books* is still of great service in tracing older books (by author or by subject) which cannot easily be found elsewhere; and the latest issue of the *Reference Catalogue*, which lists all books in print in Britain at the date of issue, is an essential part of a Readers' Adviser's collection.

No bibliography, however out-of-date it may appear, should be thrown away: it may not warrant a place at the Readers' Adviser's desk, but it is certainly worth keeping in reserve stock, for many enquiries relate to books long forgotten and the older bibliographies may be the only surviving record of their publication. It should also be considered whether space can be found for a collection of pamphlet bibliographies. Such an adjunct is easy to build up, is comparatively inexpensive, and is especially suitable for small libraries which cannot afford the more costly bibliographies: the main costs to the library are the storage cabinet or boxes and the space involved. A collection of pamphlet bibliographies can include anything which gives accurate information on publications on a subject or of a writer: thus, on birds, a bookseller's or an auctioneer's catalogue of valuable ornithological works of the eighteenth century, a supplement of the *School Library Review* containing a list of books on birds, and the Science library's bibliography on the Flight of Birds, would constitute a good beginning for a section on this subject. Many booksellers issue excellent subject-catalogues which are informal bibliographies, and with the bibliographies issued by the National Book League, the British Council, etc., a valuable working tool can be built up at very little cost. A glance at Mr F. Seymour Smith's notable *Pamphlet Bibliographies*, issued by the National Book League in 1948, will show what can be achieved in the way of effectively constructing and indexing such a collection.

Those libraries which can afford to provide the Readers' Adviser with the more substantial published bibliographies in addition, will thus arm him with his best means of serving readers. This applies even more to small than to large libraries, for where the books themselves are not available the reader is at least given constructive help by the knowledge of what has actually been issued on the subject in which he is interested. Here the published catalogues of special libraries—more particularly those of the London Library, the Royal Institute of British Architects, the National Union of Teachers, the Music Department of Liverpool Public Libraries, Dr Williams's Library, etc., and the *London Bibliography of the Social Sciences*—can be of the greatest service, since their high standards of book selection guide the reader to the worth-while material.

An important branch of the Adviser's printed aids is the great range of indexes of periodical literature. Though most of them are American their use is justified in Britain for the majority of the periodicals they index are to be found, if not in the average public library, at least in the appropriate special and government libraries, and some—like the *Engineering Index*—have an international coverage. For general periodicals the British Library Association's annual *British Humanities Index* (with quarterly supplements) and its monthly *British Technology Index* (cumulating annually), and the American *Reader's Guide to Periodical Literature* and the *International Index* will cover most of the outstanding weeklies, monthlies and quarterlies. For technical periodicals there are the *Applied Science and Technology Index* and the *Engineering Index*, the latter including summaries, and having an index of authors. For political, sociological and international issues it is essential to subscribe to the *Public Affairs Information Service*, a weekly cumulating index which covers much international, government and non-commercial pamphlet and report material which it would be difficult to trace elsewhere. For biographical material in both books and periodicals there is the excellent *Biography Index*—the *Essay and General Literature Index* also included material on this subject before 1946.

In addition, there are many specialized indexes of material on Agriculture, Art, Bibliography, Education, Law, Medicine, etc., which are of great value if the library concerned has a sufficiently representative collection of periodicals on these subjects.

Several of the government departments and international bodies issue special lists of important periodical articles in their field: notable among these are the Ministry of Works, the Ministry of Health, and the United Nations Library. Nor should the authoritative bibliographies of special subjects—containing both book and periodical article references—issued by the House of Commons Library and the Legislative Reference Services of the Library of Congress and the Australian National Library at Canberra be overlooked: these could form part of the pamphlet bibliographies collection, but are better catalogued separately and given a temporary binding so that they can be shelved with the larger bibliographies on the same subject.

For the older publications the Adviser will need to have access to the old and new catalogues of the British Museum, to the catalogues of the Library of Congress and the Bibliothèque Nationale, and to the national bibliographies of the more important countries.

To answer the many enquiries concerning what periodicals are available on specific subjects it is necessary to have up-to-date copies of the *Newspaper Press Directory* and *Willing's Press Guide* (and its quarterly supplements) for British, and Ayer's for North American periodicals, while Ulrich provides the best selective list of English-language and foreign periodicals grouped together by subject.

Finally, no Readers' Adviser's desk should lack copies of *Whitaker's Almanack*, the *Concise Oxford Dictionary*, *Who's Who*, Chambers's or Webster's *Biographical Dictionary*, an up-to-date atlas and gazetteer, and the *Oxford Companions to English, French, and American Literature*, together with a copy of the classification in use in his library, and Dr A. J. Walford's excellent *Guide to Reference Material* (and its Supplements).

The Library Handbook

NO library service is complete without its handbook giving details of its resources and services and the way to make the fullest use of them. The production of a handbook entails much care in its preparation and considerable expense in its printing if it is comprehensive. Nevertheless a well-written handbook carefully distributed will prove of great use to serious readers and aid many who would hesitate to ask for personal help.

The points to be covered in the handbook are:

(a) addresses, phone numbers, hours of opening and names of all departments and branches of the library service;

(b) a brief but interesting description of the resources of the library system and their division between the different departments, branches and special collections;

(c) an explanation of the system of classification in use;

(*d*) an explanation, with examples, of how to use the catalogues;

(*e*) an explanation of how to find a book on the shelves;

(*f*) a description of the library system in detail, department by department, with plans of the principal rooms;

(*g*) an explanation of how to obtain books not on the shelves, by reservation, use of the interloan system, etc.

(*h*) a brief summary of the rules of the library—mainly from the point of view of what may be done, rather than what is forbidden—and especially how to become a member;

(*i*) a map of the district, showing the position of every library and service point;

(*j*) a brief history of the library system;

(*k*) a brief account of stock and issues—pictorial rather than statistical;

(*l*) details of any extension activities—lectures, courses, concerts, etc.

(*m*) details of any other library publications available, with prices;

(*n*) an invitation to ask the staff for help;

(*o*) an introduction to the local collection and local history in general;

(*p*) details (including prices) of copying and reproduction services;

(*r*) availability of microfilm and microcard readers, and any other special equipment (such as an illuminated table for the examination of maps, listening room for gramophone records and tapes, etc.);

(*s*) interavailability of readers' tickets, holiday facilities, etc.

The handbook should be the co-operative effort of the whole staff: a skeleton outline should first be prepared by the Readers' Adviser, and copies should then be circulated to members of the staff with invitations to comment freely. The resulting criticisms, additions and suggestions should be tabulated, discussed at the next staff meeting and incorporated in accordance with that meeting's decisions. The final draft should be circulated to members of the Library Committee with the Agenda for approval at the Committee's next meeting and then sent to the printer. This appears to be a long-winded method of preparing a handbook, but it must be remembered that it will be used by people with very varying attitudes and standards of intelligence: the more advance criticisms, therefore, which can be obtained and met, the better chance the handbook has of being truly effective. A remarkable example of a skilfully written and illustrated and very successful handbook can be seen in the annual *Know Your Library*, issued by the Library of the University of California at Lost Angeles (UCLA).

Handbooks for the use of the Junior, Intermediate, and other departments should also be prepared wherever possible. The approach of these should be modified to suit their particular audiences.

While, theoretically, it would be more economical and efficient to produce such a handbook co-operatively on a national basis, in actual practice it could not take the place of the probably inferior but *local* product which gives due emphasis to local considerations and interests and has much the same advantage as the local over the national newspaper even in things quite outside its usual scope.

Bulletins and Booklists

THE smallest of booklists is of help to readers, for a library, even when it is almost empty, is overwhelming to the reader who may spend only ten or twenty minutes in it on each visit. The opportunity which a list gives to a reader of studying its contents at his leisure at home is an invaluable service. Even if the library issues only a duplicated list of books without any explanation of their contents, it has made a considerable advance on the library which issues nothing: a point amply demonstrated when the early county libraries issued their first catalogues.

The most usual and the most useful form of booklist is the bulletin, issued regularly, in which the library reports its principal recent additions and adds notes and news of developments in its service. Bulletins vary from simple folders to quite large magazines, but their purpose is the same: to keep the reader in touch with the best of the world's books and other publications as they appear. To this end some libraries include articles by specialists on special subjects as a means of introducing their readers to the standard works on the subject, or to new works in the same field. Other features often included are:

(1) a list of the libraries with their addresses, hours of opening and telephone numbers;

(2) notes of any changes in the library's services;

(3) announcements of any extension activities such as lectures, exhibitions, concerts, etc.

(4) children's page (where no separate children's bulletin is issued;

(5) reminder of various facilities offered by the library (renewals by telephone, obtaining books from other libraries, special materials—such as original paintings and drawings —available for loan, holiday facilities, etc.)

(6) illustrations—such as outstanding illustrations from books listed in the current number, portraits of local people, illustrations of local scenes, etc.

but additional matter—especially special articles—should not be allowed to overshadow the booklists so much that the reader will be inclined to overlook the latter.

Some librarians prefer to issue special booklists devoted to individual subjects or groups of related subjects instead of regular bulletins of recent additions, and others issue them in addition to a monthly bulletin. The booklist on a special subject has a different appeal from that of the bulletin—almost everyone will take home a copy of the bulletin in the hope it may contain notes of one or two books which will interest him. In this way, a reader is often introduced to a subject new to him simply by its being mentioned in the bulletin. On the other hand, a booklist is able to give far more detailed attention to a single subject, so that the main holdings of the library in that field are fairly shown. It has also the advantage that the booklist will probably reach the limited number of people who are interested in the subject, since few people who are not will bother to take away a copy. On the other hand, if bulletins are not issued, perhaps only one booklist may be issued during the course of any one year which will appeal to an individual reader, so that the regular impact of the bulletin is lost. The ideal seems to be either to issue both bulletins and booklists, or to combine them both and issue booklists as part of the bulletin. In any case, a booklist is invaluable even to the regular reader since it draws to his attention books which, either because they are popular or because they are in reserve stock, never appear on the shelves.

With both booklists and bulletins it is necessary to determine in advance two important questions. First of all, whether they should be comprehensive or selective. There are definite advantages to be gained from the comprehensive booklist or bulletin since these act in fact as auxiliary catalogues, putting into the reader's hands a full survey of a section of the library's resources. On the other hand, the listing of all the material added to a library during a particular period or on a particular subject usually involves so many entries for individual items that it is not possible to give more than a brief entry for each, without the annotation which would distinguish one book from another with a similar name. Moreover, the large number of popular and specialized items tend to obscure the few books of real worth. The selective list or bulletin has the merit of being able to devote far more space to each item and therefore to give the reader some idea of it so that he can decide whether this book really suits his needs. On the other hand, there is the disadvantage that the selective list concentrates all the demand on a limited number of items, a demand which is artificial to a certain extent since many readers might be content to have other titles on the same subject.

There is a distinct case for providing, if possible, both the selective and comprehensive forms, since each appeals to a different audience, just as some railway users need only a leaflet while others buy a full-scale timetable each month. It is also necessary to consider in advance the arrangement of the booklists and bulletins to be issued: most libraries develop a form of arrangement of contents which suits their readers and then keep to that system except on special occasions. A few libraries deliberately experiment with changes in arrangement (especially where items are grouped in loose subject form) in order to interest readers in new subjects. Whatever policy is adopted, the plan should be thought out in advance, since it will have some bearing on the space available for annotations, etc., and also on questions of layout, printing costs and other production details which are discussed in a later chapter (see page 48).

Some years before the war the possibility of issuing books and bulletins on a national co-operative basis was discussed and later put into effect. It was, for instance, quite absurd that on such occasions as a Coronation some five or six hundred libraries should each issue a booklist, most of them containing much the same material but with a very varying level of production and appearance when, by co-operative effort on a national basis, a booklist of high standard and far superior quality of production and appeal could be produced more cheaply. The Association of Assistant Librarians issued a monthly annotated bulletin of the best books of the month, and the County Libraries Section of the Library Association published an excellent series of short booklists on various subjects. Since the war both the Library Association and its County Libraries Section have issued subject lists of a high quality of production and book selection, and the public's reaction to them has been very encouraging.

Nevertheless, there will still be room and need for the individual booklist produced locally, for many subjects and their aspects have a purely local interest or a demand which may be more intense in one region than in another. But even such lists should, wherever possible, be produced co-operatively with the active participation of local interested bodies—not only libraries, but chambers of commerce, museums, individual manufacturers, and any other sources from which help can willingly be elicited, and it should be remembered that it is through such channels that non-readers may ultimately be reached by careful distribution of these publications.

Catalogues, Bibliographies and other Printed Matter

FROM time to time most libraries find themselves in the position of having to issue something rather more ambitious than a bulletin or a booklist. The days when almost every library was obliged, because of the indicator system of issue, to publish a printed catalogue and frequent supplements have long passed, and although Glasgow, Manchester and Bristol continue to issue a series of splendid classified catalogues, and the London Library's author and subject catalogues are still appearing, few libraries appear willing to follow Westminster's example in reverting to the printed form. There have however been many examples of quite detailed catalogues of local collections, notably those of Birmingham and Gloucester, and recently several county libraries have produced less bulky but yet able catalogues of material related to their regions. In addition, there is a growing movement on the part of libraries to produce scholarly bibliographies of local worthies, such as Sheffield's on Robert Owen.

Even the smallest library is occasionally called upon to compile comprehensive bibliographies of special subjects. Various aspects of local history form the basis for many of these, while special subjects of topical interest—such as a royal wedding, a general election, or other events of national importance—create special demands for comprehensive treatment. The detailed bibliographies issued by the National Book League are invaluable to libraries, and most of them become institutional members of the League and make its publications available to their readers. These, with the bibliographies issued by other important public bodies such as the British Council, form both excellent source material and good models for a library's own efforts and are well worth careful study.

Every piece of printed material issued by a library should be a worthy ambassador of the service available to readers. Overdue and reserve notices should be well printed, and should bear such items as telephone numbers, hours of opening and any other information which is of definite help to readers. Bookplates should be attractively designed, and should be worded as informally and helpfully as possible. There are two ways of wording the summary of rules and facilities which appears on most bookplates: one is to couch everything in a negative fashion, detailing what a reader cannot or must not do. The more palatable way— and one which will usually elicit a very much better response— is to tell the reader what he *may* do. Thus one can either say: "This book must be returned within fourteen days of the date of issue unless renewed ...", or "If you wish to keep this book beyond the normal period, please apply for a renewal ..." As far as possible, negatives are best avoided: thus, instead of "Do not misuse this book" it is preferable to say "Please take care of this book". In these days it is better to use the second rather than the third person: thus, "books which are already on loan may be reserved ..." can be phrased more effectively as "you may reserve any book which is ..." In fact, the more informal and helpful the wording the more the reader is likely to read and take notice of it.

Membership forms are even nowadays often crowded with small print which few new readers bother to read. A leaf can be taken here from the book of the transport companies who print only essential information on their tickets and refer their customers to the printed regulations exhibited elsewhere.

In the same way, the by-laws and regulations of the library need not be printed in the style of the usual mass of print exhibited at the entrances to public parks. Well set out and printed they will no longer mar the impression received by the reader as he enters the library. The thoughtful reader realizes the necessity for rules in any public service and will often plough through them in search of the facilities which can help him.

Every book, reader's ticket and notice issued by a library should bear an invitation to the reader to ask for further help and information.

Annotations

EVEN the barest list of books is of considerable aid to readers in their use of the library. Each additional detail—such as date, publisher, size, number of pages and illustrations, etc.—increases the assistance to readers. If to these items is added a brief annotation—a description and evaluation of the book—the list becomes invaluable.

The writing of annotations is very nearly an art: it is certainly not an easy task to undertake, and it is one which necessitates a wide knowledge of books and life, and an economical style. An annotation, if it is to be a just description of the book, requires detailed study of the contents of the volume from the point of view of possible readers—it cannot be satisfactorily constructed from a publisher's blurb or even from a good review intended for a different audience (although these are the sources of too many so-called annotations). Occasionally a quotation from a review will help to explain an obscure title or to reveal the author's unusual treatment of a subject, but usually the annotation must be specially written to suit the individual needs of the locality in which the library is situate.

The ideas of different annotators on the practice of their work vary very considerably as is shown in the following three examples (from different publications) of examples of annotations of John Fischer's *The Scared Men in the Kremlin* (Hamish Hamilton, 1947, 10s. 6d.):

"The author, since 1933, has studied Russian history and power relationships. For two months in 1946, he was a member of a mission to Russia. He here examines the working of the

Soviet system and attempts 'to estimate how that system is likely to behave under the pressure of a new and still unstable balance of power.'—*Foreword*." Croydon Public Libraries Readers' Index and Guide, October—December, 1947, p. 79.

"An attempt to explain the motives behind present Russian foreign policy. Based on a study of Russian history made during the last fourteen years." Norwich Public Libraries. Readers' Guide, October—December, 1947, p. 158.

"Author records his impressions and observations of a visit to the Ukraine in the spring of last year, together with his views of the motives of Soviet policy at the present day." Halifax Public Libraries. The Halifax Reader, October, 1947, p. 27.

It will at once be noticed that the Halifax annotation gives a very different impression of the book from that given by Croydon and Norwich. Another noticeable characteristic is that Croydon prefers to quote from the foreword, whereas the other two libraries give very much briefer annotations which describe the purpose of the book in a more general fashion.

It is certain that no two librarians will agree entirely on what the annotation of any particular book should comprise, but their aim in all cases is to give the reader a clear and unbiased idea of the subject and purpose of the book, and the degree of success which the author has achieved in his task. At the same time it is not necessary to emphasize the obvious: the author's qualifications for writing the book are of interest, but the very fact that the book appears in the library's list should be sufficient indication that the author's credentials were investigated by the staff before his book was recommended for purchase. Again, the annotation need not paraphrase information already contained in the title. The recommended maximum of thirty words for an annotation is sometimes taken as a minimum as well, whereas the minimum should be just so much as will describe the book adequately, whether it takes three or thirty words (or more) to do so.

Rather should the annotator assume that the addition of the

book to the library's stock guarantees it to be a worth-while contribution to the subject, and that everything must be done to encourage members of the library to read it. To this end, he should carefully consider:

(a) the specific requirements and interests of readers in the area—which may in themselves determine a style of annotation very different from that suitable for a library system a few miles away;

(b) current events and interests which have any connection with the author or subject-matter of the book. Thus a book on capital punishment would be described as of interest in connection with the renewed attempts to abolish the capital sentence in Great Britain.

Annotations for the bulletin and for the printed or card catalogues are not necessarily subject to the same rules. In the bulletin it is permissible to make topical allusions, secure in the assurance that they will be understood by everyone. In annotating for the more permanent catalogues such an assurance is unwarranted, and care should be taken to write what can be just as easily understood in six years' as in six months' time.

The following points should be observed when annotating books in the various classes:

Philosophy and Psychology: Classify philosophical works by schools of thought, and indicate their relation to previous or contemporary theorists. Psychological and psycho-analytical works in particular require this information, since differences of opinion among the leading exponents of these subjects are of the greatest importance. The degree of preliminary knowledge needed by the reader should be stated.

Religion: The religious standpoint of the author should be clearly stated, and the religion discussed should also be identified. The type of reader addressed must also be shown.

Sociology: Books on politics and international affairs require the standpoint of the author and perhaps his political standing and period. Economic works must be differentiated into grades of specialization, and theories masquerading as accepted principles must be unmasked. Legal works need classification into textbook, treatise and popular types. Costume books should be assessed at their true value from the points of view of the artist, the amateur dress-designer, and the dramatic producer, as well as from the standpoint of the historian. In education, as in all the books in this class, foreign (such as American) treatment needs to be noted.

Philology: Books on languages should show whether they are historical, comparative, conversational, or direct method. Previous knowledge needed should be stated, and other material required—such as readers or grammars, gramophone records, tapes, pictures, etc.—should be indicated.

Science and Technical Works: Previous knowledge needed must be stated. Foreign (e.g. American) treatment should be shown. Illustrations and tables should be assessed at their practical worth to the reader without access to the laboratory or the workshop.

Art: Books on art rely on illustrations for much of their effect, and the processes by which the illustrations are reproduced—and the use of colour—are especially worth noting. Often a note on the nationality and school of the artist is necessary.

Literature: Classical works need the language in which they are written, the period treated, the presence of notes and critical apparatus as well as the particular text in use. Notes on the author and his relation to the literary developments of his country are especially important in the case of foreign (and more particularly, contemporary) works.

History: Historical works may possess some special viewpoint or they may relate to some, at first, unidentified period. Fanciful titles especially need explanation. Special appendices, chronologies and genealogies may merit notice. Previous knowledge needed for geographical and historical treatises should be stated. Modern editions of standard travel works sometimes lack the original maps or illustrations—a fact which is as important to note as any modification or abridgment of the text.

The absence of an index in the case of all serious works should always be noted.

These are but the barest notes on the annotation of special classes of books to which any experienced cataloguer will add many more from his own experience. The only guide in cases of doubt must be the true interests of the library's own readers.

Notices

IN spite of the many attempts to improve the standard of notices in libraries, many of them fail to avoid the institutional impression they are at so much pains to remove. The purpose of a notice is to inform clearly and with as little fuss as possible: the best way to achieve this is to have good presentation. An excellent example of good notice design is that employed by the National Gallery where even such injunctions as DO NOT SMOKE are given a positively attractive air. The pleasant effect which the National Gallery has succeeded in introducing is due to:

(1) good lettering;
(2) simple but skilful lay-out and the use of colour;
(3) framing in attractive picture-frames and making them part of the general colour scheme;
(4) effective wording.

Even modern aids to lettering can reduce a notice to humdrum appearance when used by unskilful or unimaginative assistants. Stencils are often used without any reference to the general principles of good lay-out or to the current standards for the mixture of colours or type founts. Margins are often reduced out of all proportion to the type area which they surround: more usually they are unbalanced in relation to the reading matter. Sometimes unsuitable paper is used. Very often the crest of the corporation or organization is affixed to every notice without reference to its suitability: still more regularly the name of the organization sprawls across the head of every notice, obscuring the importance of the actual words describing the subject of the notice.

The same considerations apply to the printed notices commissioned by libraries. Printed notices in libraries are usually confined to by-laws, regulations, notices of lectures, concerts, exhibitions, and directions to different departments. Little attention is paid to such fugitive material and their general effect is uninviting.

In these days of mass advertising when notices and advertisements shout at the public from every hoarding, the human eye has become accustomed to reject automatically and unconsciously most of the unaesthetic items which meet its gaze. Moreover, ineffectual notices can spoil the appearance of a library and give it the very poor-law aspect which has almost disappeared elsewhere. The ubiquity of black-and-white notices in ugly type surrounded by thin black frames breeds dislike in the reader's mind.

This is no plea for a preciousness in the design of notices which would have an equally bad effect. A notice should simply be well designed with good type, good colouring, good lay-out, and effective presentation, so that it shall appeal to, rather than offend the reader's best instincts. This entails the close scrutiny of each notice, before it is exhibited, from the point of view of the reader, and the refusal to tolerate poor or shoddy work or inappropriate wording. If this is done, the reader will indeed have been helped, for a well-guided library with clear, concise and friendly notices is appreciated as much by the leisurely as by the hurried visitor to the library.

Publicity

THE library is of no use to the reader if he is unaware of its existence: many a would-be reader, for instance, passes within a hundred yards or so of his local public library without knowing that it is there. In the same way, readers who are well aware of their library are often not at all familiar with its resources, and there cannot be too much publicity in as many different media as possible to bring the library to the notice of the many people it is able to serve.

Since libraries are so often tucked away in the less-frequented parts of towns or of buildings, it is essential to see that notices directing readers to them start from the busiest points and are repeated at every stage where there are two or more different turnings. That this is necessary can be shown from the fact that members of the senior staff of more than one important official organization have remained ignorant of the existence of a good library in their own building and have appealed to outside agencies for information which was almost literally at their elbow. In addition, there should be permanent notices concerning the library and its position (together with clear sketch maps or plans) at all central points where they may be of use to strangers as well. The repetition of a marked plan on the more substantial printed matter issued by the library is also advisable, since the readers who find such publications useful are the very people who may wish to visit the library in person.

Once it has been ensured that every effort has been made to make known the existence and position of the library to all who are likely to wish to make use of it, attention can be turned to more detailed publicity. Maps, plans, directories and other matter published independently should be checked each time a new issue is published to see whether the library is correctly indicated and described, and where no entry is given, contact should be made with the publisher to make certain that future editions are provided with entries. Telephone directories, for instance, very often contain the name of the authority or organization controlling the library without specific mention of the latter: an additional entry for the library and its branches (including street names and numbers) will save many times its cost in speed and service.

Regular lists (preferably annotated) of recent additions should be sent to the local press, house organs, or any other journal which reaches potential readers. Brief lists are more likely to be printed, and if these can be cast in the form of an article they are more attractive to the reader. In the *Observer* which for many years has been short of space for book reviews, attention has been focused each Sunday on four or five titles of books for which no room for a more detailed notice has been found: there is little doubt that the *Observer*'s readers have become accustomed to taking especial notice of that list each week, since they have realized that great care has been taken in its selection—a lesson which could well be learnt by all writers who bewail the little space given to them in printed journals.

A rather more indirect form of publicity of this type is the news or statistical item put into the form of a brief news paragraph which editors can use for filling a short column: many of these will not of course be used, but if they are sent out regularly those which are printed will help to focus attention on the library. To be effective, however, they must be clear, topical and of general appeal. In public libraries the chief source of such items is the local collection.

There are other opportunities for publicity which are sometimes not fully exploited. Exhibitions, lectures, demonstrations, concerts, agricultural and flower shows, and many other events held at some distance from the library can be utilised by the provision of suitable stands or publicity matter or even printed booklists and small collections of appropriate books and periodicals. In this connection, close contact should always be maintained with local associations and societies of all descriptions, so that no opportunity is lost of providing help to them—and thus further publicity for the library—whenever possible. Special displays in shops can sometimes be linked with the library by the inclusion of exhibits of relevant books: the special question of Book Weeks will be discussed in a later chapter (see page 92).

One of the best forms of publicity is the personal contact which is made and maintained between librarian and public. Librarians and all members of their staffs should seize every chance of addressing groups—large or small—on the subject of books,

47

libraries in general, or their own particular library. Talks to small groups of people having a common interest—such as gatherings of people engaged in the same trade or profession—are the most effective, since the questions which follow the talk will be of interest to all present and will stimulate more detailed discussion of the subject than would be possible in a more general audience.

The maintenance of a file of records of readers' interests, grouped under specific subjects, is of great publicity value, since it is possible with such a list to put the people most concerned in direct touch with any outstanding book or periodical article which has been added to the library, and thus perhaps revive interest among those readers who may feel that they have exhausted the resources of the library in the field which interests them.

The aim of the librarian and his staff is to make the library an accepted part of his readers' life so that they feel inclined to appeal to it for assistance whenever they are faced with problems which published information may help to solve. If publicity is to be truly effective and not to play the rôle of a boomerang, it must not only be well designed with a particular audience kept well in mind, but it must also be backed with adequate staff and resources ready to carry out the promises and opportunities it broadcasts. Publicity therefore needs careful planning, and no premature notice of a service should ever be issued, since a potential reader who is disappointed on his first approach to the library is hardly likely to try to make use of it at any later time.

Print and Production

THE resources of print and paper, design and lay-out, available to different libraries vary enormously even between libraries which are near to each other. The only limiting factors are those imposed by the needs (and the finance) of the individual library. Before any decision on the form can be taken, it is however necesary to examine the purpose which the publication is to fulfil.

Thus, in the case of a bulletin or a booklist, it is essential to determine how frequently it is to be published, whether it is to be sold or given away free of charge—if the latter, whether circulation is to be restricted to particular groups of people—whether it should take the form of a bookmark, a booklet or a leaflet, whether advertisements and illustrations are to be included (in which case, provision must be made for suitable paper and for blocks), and what approximate size is envisaged. The last point is especially important wherever it is proposed to send out a large number of copies by post, since the difference of half an inch or so may make all the difference between a comparatively cheap and a very much more expensive envelope, according to whether the size conforms with accepted commercial sizes or not. The final and most important point is the question of the number of copies required: if only two or three hundred copies of a specialized booklist are needed, it should be considered whether it would not be adequate to duplicate it or to produce it in some less expensive way than by having it printed. Whenever very large quantities are wanted, print is naturally the most satisfactory medium.

In the case of printed material, other points which will need to be settled are the approximate number of pages, the type to be used, the date by which the material is needed, and estimates of the cost. Most of these items are best determined in collaboration with the printer, whose advice on what is and what is not technically possible is essential. Nevertheless, good standards should be insisted upon: whatever types the local printer has immediately available, he is in a position nowadays to have the copy set up in a more suitable fount since the developments of the last few years have put within the printer's reach a wide range of good founts from the big type corporations. In the same way, questions of choice of paper, method of binding—sewing, stapling, etc.— are now becoming less difficult to solve.

Except in cases where printed matter is needed urgently, it is usual to ask for estimates from two or three different firms. Thus a printer might be asked to submit his estimate for printing:

1,500 copies of an 8-page booklist on Sports and Games. Royal 8vo. Contents to be printed in 10-pt. Times Roman on antique paper (as copy attached). 4-page good quality art-paper cover for taking 120-screen block (to be supplied). Booklist to be stapled. Both galley and page proofs will be needed, and the completed product must be delivered by 20th May, 1963.

Here the printer would be asked to submit with his estimate samples of the paper and cover paper which he proposed to use. To try to pin down a good printer to a more rigid set of conditions is to court, if not disaster, at least very mediocre work. Within the general limits laid down for the tender the printer should be encouraged at every point to use his greater experience in the production of the library's publications. The librarian is, after all, at best only an amateur, whereas the printer will often recognize instantly possibilities unsuspected by the librarian.

While it is not possible or even desirable to give a list of the only types suitable for library publications, some indication of what can be relied upon to present a good appearance can be given by naming some of the most acceptable types in use to-day: Times Roman is probably the most popular at the present time, while Bembo, Caslon, Baskerville, Garamond, Bodoni, Gill Sans, Perpetua and Walbaum provide a sufficient range for the variations which might be needed to differentiate the publications of the average library. Thus this book is set in 11 on 12-pt. Bembo, with an average of 38 lines (including the running-title and the page-number) to the page. The size of the book is large crown octavo, and the paper used is Dalmore Smooth Cartridge 32 × 42 inches, each ream of 516 sheets weighing 85 lbs.

Once the tender has been accepted the librarian should confine his activities to providing "clean" copy and to efficient proof-reading. Large additions and deletions, once the material has reached the galley-proof stage, can spoil the lay-out and tend to make the printer lose interest. "Author's corrections" caused by faulty copy can also occasion heavy charges for the printer's time. Careful proof-reading will eliminate embarrassing or humorous misprints which would detract from the value of an otherwise excellent publication. A single howler can completely spoil the force of a powerful argument for more staff or a larger book-fund.

Especial care should be paid to the reproduction of illustrations. Proofs of illustrations are usually hand-pulls made by the block-maker himself on better quality paper than will be used in the actual publication. By producing these pulls by hand, the experienced block-maker is able to provide a better impression than will afterwards be produced when the block is locked in the forme and printed by mechanical means. Every care should be taken to ensure that the illustrations are reproduced as carefully and clearly as the printer can possibly manage.

All publications issued by the library should bear on them the name and address of the library. In the case of handbills, leaflets and posters announcing events of any description, especial care should be taken to ensure that exact details of time, place, conditions of admission, etc., are included, and a sketch map should be given if the place is at all difficult to find. It is also a very good system to award a serial number and date to each publication issued by the library. In the course of time copies of library publications often stray far away and it is essential that their readers should be able to identify them. There is also the great advantage of ease and accuracy of reference which a serial number gives. The inclusion of the date is also of great importance since statements are only true at the date at which they are made: for instance, hours of opening, addresses, telephone numbers and names of officials are all liable to change, and the reader is helped by a date which enables him to estimate how accurate the information given is likely to be now. The inclusion of the name and address of the publisher is also of importance: thus it is impossible to identify the official directory of more than one large town, owing to their being given a publisher's name such as "Thomas's Almanac", except by such internal evidence as advertisements and street names may provide.

Though imitation is never acceptable to the progressive librarian, it is useful to be able to show the printer one or two examples of other publications as the type of production the librarian has in mind, and for this—among other purposes—it is a wise policy to collect and keep a good file of the publications of the more important libraries at home and abroad. Excellent examples of well-printed annual reports, booklists, lecture lists, etc., can be obtained from such public libraries as Bristol, Finchley, Hampstead, Hendon, Hornsey, Leeds, Liverpool, Glasgow, Rugby, Sheffield, etc.

Part III

ADVISORY WORK WITH READERS

Readers' Advisory Service

THE job of Readers' Adviser is one of the most attractive of the many different kinds of work in librarianship. It is a job for the true bookman with a wide knowledge of books and life and a real liking for helping other people. There are no riches to be gained in the Readers' Advisory Service: unfortunately, in present-day librarianship it is necessary to become an administrative officer in order to reach the higher salary grades, and many a librarian and deputy librarian find that their work consists more of committee duties, superintending buildings and repairs, staff and finance, than of selecting books and helping readers. The situation will no doubt be more clearly defined in the future and, in the meantime, many librarians will continue to select readers' advisory work or reference librarianship as some of the most satisfying branches of modern work in libraries.

Before a Readers' Advisory Service is made available to the public it should be very carefully organized. The desk of the Readers' Adviser should be placed in such a position that it is easily accessible to the readers while, at the same time, it does not impede their passage from one section of the library to another. If the desk is placed too near the shelves it is certain that that section will be less used by readers who will hesitate to edge between the two. If possible, the desk should be placed in the centre of a fairly open space where the readers can circulate freely, and the Readers' Adviser should sit facing the entrance to the library so that he can immediately offer to help new readers. For similar reasons the catalogues should be, if not next to his desk, at least well within his sight. At one side of the desk there should be a small bookcase capable of holding essential bibliographical reference tools.

The desk of the Readers' Adviser should be equipped with a telephone providing it is not used for receiving requests for renewals. The principle should be that the telephone is to be used mainly for outgoing calls, and for incoming calls asking for advice on reading and bibliographical information. The desk itself should be fitted to hold a small collection of files, and there should also be two or three card index drawers for information material. Where the library also has a separate house telephone, an extension should be made for the Readers' Adviser. Facing the public should be a notice inviting readers to make use of the advisory service, and the Adviser's name should be plainly displayed—readers prefer to know the name of the librarian with whom they are dealing—unless it is the custom of the library to allot readers' advisory duties to several different members of the staff at different times during the day.

New readers, after they have been registered, should be introduced to the Readers' Adviser whose job it is to discover the reader's interests and to show him where relevant material may be found on the shelves. The opportunity should be seized to give the new reader a copy of the guide to the library and any booklists which may be of help to him, or to prepare an individual reading-list if he has special requirements.

The part of the Readers' Adviser in the work of selecting books for the library must necessarily be large: in his analysis of the interests of readers he soon becomes aware of subjects which are ill-covered or totally unrepresented. In addition, if he keeps a detailed record of the tastes of new readers he will gradually become possessed of valuable information on the proportion of demand for particular subjects. This information, when collated with the detailed analysis of recent book issues, should provide a sure guide to future selection of material. The analysis of issues alone would be inadequate since it would show only the demand for subjects already represented in the library, and would be conditioned therefore by the degree of good or bad representation and by the number of books provided on each subject.

All displays and exhibits of books and the issue of reading lists and bibliographies should be the responsibility of the Readers' Adviser; this will entail his keeping in close touch with daily topics. It will be his duty as soon as he commences work each day to glance through the newspapers and to note subjects on which a sudden demand for books and other material may arise, or which may usefully be exploited by a display of the relevant printed matter in the library, and to see that this information is also passed on to other senior members of the staff. In the same way, he must keep himself informed of news of forthcoming events so that important occasions may not find the library entirely unprepared in its bookstock.

But the work of the Readers' Adviser has no bounds. His duties will include advice on markets and recent prices to readers who wish to sell or buy books, assistance to readers wishing to embark on a planned course of study or reading, helping to put readers in touch with specialist libraries where their individual needs may be more fully represented, and many more subjects which will occur (mostly unexpectedly) from day to day.

If the Readers' Adviser is to prove successful in his work, he must by nature be more of a bookman than of an administrator. There are no opportunities in Readers' Advisory work for experience in administration, and for those who are training for deputy and chief librarianships it must be regarded as an essential part of their training, but not one which will help them greatly in questions of finance, staff control, committee work or details of routine.

The Readers' Adviser must have a wide acquaintance with books in general, a thorough training in the use of bibliographical works, and a broad outlook which will enable him to give adequate attention and sympathy to all types of questions, both literary and technical, cultural and commercial.

If possible, the post of Readers' Adviser should never be held for too long by one man: it should be regarded as a special job which each of the more senior assistants should be given the opportunity of enjoying in turn—say, for twelve months at a time. There are of course great advantages in allowing the post to be retained by one assistant over a much longer period, but the arguments in its favour should not be allowed to outweigh the greater advantages of giving various members of the staff the chance to gain valuable experience and to show what they are able to do in one of the branches of librarianship which offers immense scope for originality and individuality untrammelled for the most part by considerations of routine duties, finance, or shortage of staff.

There are powerful arguments too about awarding the post of Readers' Adviser for shorter periods than a year. In the first place, it is essential that the Adviser keep himself up to date with new publications and events: thus he must read news and book reviews in both weekday and Sunday papers, scan periodicals for items on local industries and interests, go through book trade journals, publishers' catalogues and announcements, etc., look for important exhibitions, trade shows and so forth planned to take place in the near future as notified in such periodicals as *Coming Events*, keep in touch with the chief programmes and developments on radio and television, and examine new additions to the stock of all departments. For such a routine to be a success, it must be possible to assure the Readers' Adviser of a fairly lengthy period in which he may hold the post. Secondly, it is the Readers' Adviser's duty to study the general nature of the area in which he is working, to keep in touch with the activities of local industry and commerce, local societies and organizations and schools, to build up friendly relations with other libraries and sources of information, and to maintain adequate records of his work. Here again any less period than a year would defeat the purpose of such duties.

However good the Readers' Adviser, the efficiency of his work must depend on an adequate stock of standard books and periodicals and an adequate book fund. It must be dependent too on good cataloguing, classification and guiding, and on the adequacy of the staff at the main service points. It must in fact depend on the efficiency of the library system as a whole, just as the efficiency of the system depends in its turn on the way in which he carries out his duties. The moral is clear: the efficiency of any library system is a result of the combination of good staff, good stock and good organization, and a weakness in any of these three items will be reflected in the reduced ability of the library to help its readers adequately.

It is not necessary to maintain elaborate records of readers' enquiries. Most libraries find it sufficient to note on a suggestions card or enquiry form the main points concerning the book or information required, together with name, address and phone number of the reader. In many cases a serial number is written or pre-printed on the card, and a tally with the same number given to the reader, so that he can ask what progress is being made with his enquiry at any time. A weekly or half-weekly check of these forms is made, and individual decisions made whether to purchase or borrow the item asked for. Urgent items are given special treatment. When the books are received they are marked with special signals, so that their processing, etc. is not delayed, and the reader is notified as soon as possible of the availability of the material. Records of the number of enquiries, the number not satisfied, and relevant dates are kept both for statistical purposes and for guidance in future book-selection. Frequent analysis of those enquiries not satisfied is essential from the point of view of maintaining an adequate stock.

Notification Postcard

BOROUGH OF HORNSEY PUBLIC LIBRARIES

You may be interested in the books mentioned below on the subject which you are studying which have been added to the Libraries.

Any of these books will be reserved for you on request.

W. B. STEVENSON,
Borough Librarian.

No...............................

HORNSEY PUBLIC LIBRARIES

READER'S ENQUIRY FORM

Book, publication or subject required.
(Please give fullest possible particulars)

Author..

Title or subject ....

Publisher .... *Date of publication*...............

Price .... *B.N.B. No*...........................

Name of Enquirer ....

Address ....

....

The fee for reserving a book is threepence. If it is necessary to borrow a book from another library an additional ninepence to cover postage is charged. Do you wish this to be done if necessary? ....

If the suggestion has been rejected, the reason is:

....

....

Multiple Purpose Form

HORNSEY PUBLIC LIBRARIES
Telephone: MOUntview 1652/9412

....

....

....

....

With reference to the above, please see paragraph............
below.

1. Your name has been added to the waiting list: available
about.......................Please inform us if you do not wish
your name to remain on the list.

2. Has been renewed until...................................

3. Cannot be renewed, and should be returned immediately.
Required by another reader.

4. Is now overdue and should be returned immediately.

5. Can only be obtained for use in Reference Library. Please
inform us by return if we should obtain on this condition.

6. We can only trace..

....

....

....

...................................Is this the work you require?

7. Please forward book: we agree to accept conditions.

8. Please cancel our application.

9. Regret not available for one of the following reasons:
   (a) Not in the library.
   (b) Out of print. If desired we will try to borrow it from another library.
      (.........................will be charged for postage.)
   (c) Not available from any co-operating library.
   (d) Cannot be traced. Please supply further details, e.g. publisher, price and date of publication.
   (e) The Public Libraries Committee regret they are unable to adopt your suggestion.
   (f) Rebinding—you will be notified when available.
   (g) Withdrawn from stock.
   (h) Not yet published. Please apply again.
   (i) Other books on the same subject are in the library and may be obtained on request.

10. Please renew for a further period.
    Last stamped date.....................Author.....................
    Title................................Class No. ... .

11. Regret your renewal application gives insufficient details. Please complete Paragraph 10 and return.

12. Recovered from.....................at a cost of..................
    Your ticket may be obtained on payment of this sum/ application.

13. The books have been received. Fines amount to...............
    (received), and your library tickets will be returned on receipt of this sum/are enclosed herewith.

Reference Method

HALF the battle in reference and information work is to discover exactly what the reader really wants. Most people are averse to stating precisely what they are looking for, and in some cases they cannot describe accurately what they want. This factor, more than any other, involves endless waste of time in searching for material which is only indirectly connected with the subject in which the reader is really interested. The fault usually lies in the fact that the reader has already made up his mind what type of book contains the answer to his query and consequently insists on seeing that volume rather than any other. If the librarian can persuade the enquirer to state his query rather than ask vaguely for a book on such and such a subject or for one obscure or unobtainable volume much time will be saved and the reader more quickly satisfied.

Not only does the librarian need to know exactly what the reader needs—in order to answer the enquiry satisfactorily he must know what kind of material, elementary, general or advanced, is required. This implies knowing what preliminary knowledge of the subject the reader already possesses. Moreover, the librarian should try to find out how detailed an answer the reader requires. Some people merely want sufficient information to enable them to settle a bet, others want a number of points to help them with a debate or an essay, while others need the utmost detail which can be discovered. If the librarian can discover these points, together with a deadline by which the reader must have his material, he stands a good chance of giving the enquirer the best service available from that particular library. Readers should be encouraged to send or 'phone their enquiries to the library in advance, wherever possible: this enables the staff to get the material ready for the reader by the time he reaches the library. This is especially important in the case of long sets of books or back files of periodicals or newspapers which have to be brought from some distant basement.

In order to answer a question accurately it is necessary to know

PLATE 1. *Telex in operation in the Commerce, Science and Technology Libraries.*

PLATE 2. *The Assize Court Library. Note the simple but well-designed and comfortable furniture.*

PLATE 3.   *Manor Branch Children's Library. Note the effective design of the display stand.*

PLATE 4.   *Firth Park Children's Library. An award being presented for the best decorated Children's Library, Christmas 1958.*

PLATE 5 & 6.   *Book display in a school, arranged by Hillsborough Branch Library.*

PLATE 7 & 8.   *Exhibition at the Library Association's 1960 Conference, incorporating the showing of two local films. A good example of a brief and clear explanation of the many activities of a large library system.*

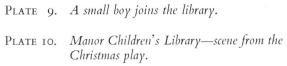

PLATE 9. *A small boy joins the library.*

PLATE 10. *Manor Children's Library—scene from the Christmas play.*

PLATE 11. *Firth Park Branch Library. The Listening Group in session.*

PLATE 12. *The Central Library Theatre.*

PLATE 13 & 14.

Manor Children's Library. Note the writing space at the catalogue; and the effective use of venetian blinds to cover the glazed partitions.

PLATE 15.
Broomhill Branch
Adult Library. Note
well-designed notices,
ledges at counter for
parcels, &c.

PLATE 16.
Woodseats Children's Library. Note the sloped shelves, with every book within easy reach.

PLATE 17.
*Woodseats Adult
Library. Note
strategic position of
staff desk in sight of
both counter and
catalogue.*

PLATE 18.

The Catalogue Department of the Los Angeles County Law Library. Note careful layout and use of small trolleys for quick processing of new items.

PLATE 19.
The Reference
Library of the Los
Angeles County Law
Library. Low island
bookcases bring
essential reference
works within easy
reach without
reducing light or
oversight.

the stock of the library thoroughly—a task which is fairly easy in a small library and almost impossible in the average medium or large collection. It is certainly easier in a small than in a large library to answer truthfully that the information is not available, for in the larger collections the resources are so vast that no one librarian can feel that he has searched them completely. Thus, every spare moment of any librarian whose duties include information or reference work is well spent in examining the material on the shelves and in the vertical file, and making sure that their contents—as well as their colour and bindings—are familiar and are kept in mind. A quarter of an hour spent in actually examining individual volumes is worth an hour of reading the excellent guides by Walford, Roberts or Winchell. Those members of the staff who are working in libraries with only a quick-reference collection should be sent regularly to nearby libraries with small but well-chosen reference stocks where they can make themselves familiar with the contents of the main reference works: if this is done, they can then often obtain information for readers over the 'phone, since they will know which libraries have the works containing the material they need.

It is especially important to examine new reference works as they are added to stock: reading reviews is not sufficient—even appraisals as carefully written as they are in the best library text-books do not give the complete picture, as many a library student has discovered during his course. When first looking at a volume it is a good system to check and compare it with other books on the same subject, noting in what respects it differs and where it adds to information already possessed by the library. The authority of the book should be studied: the author's qualifications and experience, the known reputation of the publisher in such respects as his having issued other authoritative works in this field, and the critical comments of reviews in journals devoted to the subject. The edition and the date of the original issue are also worth noting: some standard works have a tendency to retain an arrangement and method of approach which may compare unfavourably with a fresh study of the subject. The existence of errata and additions—especially if printed separately or in an obscure position in the book—and the placing of important information in appendices should be kept in mind. Illustrations, bibliographies and indexes (including the system of arrangement) should be examined, and any pronounced bias in favour of one particular theory or school of thought is worth noting. A good method is for each person who examines a reference work to write down what he has noticed and pass his comments on to his colleagues: in this way, when every member of the staff has examined the volume there will be a permanent record of the resources to be found there which can be written up, analysed for the information file, and of course passed on to new members of the staff later. In the case of periodicals it is well to be on the watch for changes of policy, contents, amalgamations, new supplements, and the many variations which can occur when a new editor takes over, or when a campaign for new subscribers causes a review of the contents. English-language material from other parts of the Commonwealth and from the United States should be studied also from the point of view of differences in spelling, approach, background, etc.

If a reader's enquiry is likely to prove extensive he should be given something to go on with while a search is made for more detailed information. Thus, if he has asked for material on recent developments in the Middle East, he should be shown the relevant portions of the index of *Keesing's* or *Facts on File*, so that he can look up references in which he is interested, while the staff are searching through periodical indexes, and examining the files of material issued by the United Nations and other government and international organizations. If the reader asks for as much information as possible on Joan of Arc, he should be given the relevant articles in the general encyclopaedias to read, while the staff search for individual biographies, passages in the larger histories, sections in the material issued by the Public Records Office, articles in historical journals and the proceedings and transactions of learned societies, etc. In short, a reader should never be left without material while the librarian goes elsewhere in search of information. The general articles in encyclopaedias and the larger reference works often bring to the attention of the reader the existence of other material on the subject through chance references in the text or through the bibliographies appended to the articles. Again, readers can be asked to examine indexes to periodicals for themselves and mark those items in which they are interested, or to glance through the relevant entries in the catalogues of the national and special libraries if they may be in a position to visit these institutions later.

After a time, the average member of the staff will be fairly certain of two points: first, whether he can answer the question himself and, secondly, whether the library contains the answer. If the assistant cannot himself cope with the enquiry he should not continue hopelessly, keeping the query to himself. He should call in the aid of other assistants in the library, so that no query ever leaves it without the whole staff (including the chief librarian, who is usually the one member of the staff who is never asked) having had a chance to help in solving the problem. Each assistant has his own interests and abilities: what may appear an insuperable difficulty to one may to another assistant prove mere child's play.

In tackling the enquiry the assistant should adopt a systematic line of approach designed to make full use of all the material in the library. The method of attack should be from the general to the particular starting from the encyclopaedias, the indexes, the bibliographies, and the standard works on the subject, and making full use of the resources of the catalogues and of the classification. Possibly the assistant may not be sufficiently familar with the subject to know where to begin: in this case he should not hesitate to ask the reader to explain to him the meaning of the subject under enquiry so that he is able to establish a satisfactory subject heading under which he can search—most readers do not expect library staffs to be possessed of encyclopaedic knowledge on every subject and are readily prepared to explain technical terms and abstruse references. In the search for useful material everything is grist to the librarian's mill: books, periodicals, pamphlets, maps, pictures, and any other material in the library. In addition, outside sources should be kept in mind, such as local experts, official departments, offices in other parts of the organization, and any other sources which can be mobilized to the library's aid, but in approaching outside sources the reader's agreement should first be obtained, in case commercial or other considerations are involved. It is essential in all but the smallest libraries to keep some record of the sources which have already been tried, for it may well be that the enquiry will be passed on to other members of the staff who will not otherwise know which items to ignore as they proceed with the search. In fact, one of the great weaknesses of the process of handling the more extended types of enquiry is the problem of adequately handing over an enquiry from one assistant to another. Unless the query is accurately described, the next assistant may look on it from a different standpoint and may produce other material than what is needed. If a suitable form is used, it can subsequently be incorporated under a suitable subject heading in the information file, or in a file of answered queries and thus be used on future occasions for other readers.

To ensure that enquiries are followed up, the reader's name and address and telephone number should be noted together with the last date the information is likely to be of use to him. Rather than wait until the enquiry has been solved completely, it is well to keep in frequent touch with the reader and give him immediately what material has come to light. This achieves two objects: first, it assures the reader that his enquiry is still progressing, and, secondly, it gives him the chance to call off the enquiry if he has obtained the information elsewhere—a frequent occurrence, since readers often put the same enquiry to several libraries at the same time.

If the assistant finally comes to the conclusion that the library cannot itself furnish the answer to a query, he should consider where else it may be found. Britain has for its size probably more library resources available than any other country in the world.

The assistant should not hesitate to approach outside sources. He should first of all ascertain from the library's own information file, or from such general reference works as the *Libraries, Museums and Art Galleries Year Book* (new edition in preparation) or the latest edition of the *ASLIB Directory* which libraries and organizations specialize in the particular subject of the enquiry. He should then telephone or write to them and state his query,

---

Subject Enquiry Form—Westminster Central Reference Library

Subject of Enquiry ....

....

....

....

.... Last date of use...........................

Date ....   Name ....

                             Address ....

                             ....

                             Phone ....

ALA Port	CBL	Gregory
Ayer	Chambers's	Hastings
BNB	DNB	Italiana
Brockhaus	Ency Am	Larousse
Catalogue	Ency Brit	L of C
CBI	Eng Cat	Lulop

Meyer	Schweizer
N & Q	Sci Museum
Nat Geog	Seligman
OED	Ulrich
Rees	Winkler Prins
Ref Cat	Wld List

having first decided in his own mind that it is the kind of enquiry which can be answered by phone or post and not one in which the reader must personally get in touch with the specialist collection. If he feels that the reader should deal direct with the specialist organization, then it is the assistant's duty to discover whether the reader may make use of that library and, if so, when and on what terms. Nothing should be taken for granted, whether library or reader approaches the outside organization, and no reader should be told that such-and-such a library has a collection of books, etc., on his subject, before the assistant has made certain that the library is still in existence, that it still specializes in that subject, that it is still at the address given in the directory and that it is not at that precise moment closed for repair, decorating, stocktaking or any other cause. The utmost effort should be made to see that the reader gets the information he needs when he wants it and in the form he desires. Equal efforts should be made to ensure that the reader does not abuse the facilities offered to him by the specialist library, so that the pitch may not be queered for the next reader for whom the library wishes to obtain an entrée. Throughout the process of solving a query no effort should be spared to make it as speedy as possible, both in the interests of the reader and in the endeavour to make the aid of the library available to as many readers as possible.

Every assistant should make an effort to get to know the resources of the libraries immediately in his neighbourhood. It is true that most staffs have little spare time in which to visit nearby libraries, but opportunities do occur from time to time at professional meetings, and on such occasions as personal visits to collect or return valuable material or to check up or copy information. One specialist library in London makes it a practice to send each member of its staff on a visit to one other library every month: the scheme is a success for it does not prove very much of a burden on the routine work of the library and it has resulted in a considerable broadening of the assistants' outlook. Any time which can be spent in visiting other libraries will produce good results, for other libraries always have some items which could usefully be noted for addition to one's own, and the interchange of ideas and experiences in librarianship often helps to solve difficult queries and to anticipate others.

Periodicals should be exploited to the full, for nowadays they are usually in advance of books in the recording of modern developments and inventions. Many a query of topical interest can be answered from *The Times* and its indexes, or from Keesing's *Contemporary Archives* or *Facts on File*. The fullest use should be made of periodicals' indexes, both British and American. If the library does not subscribe to any of these, the necessary references can very often be obtained from a nearby specialist or large general library which takes them, or from the National Central Library. Even references to periodicals not taken by the library should be noted, for they may be available in other libraries near by, or the reader may himself have access to them through his own professional or trade organization. There is also the possibility of obtaining Photostat copies of articles in specialist periodicals by means of services such as that operated by the Science Library, or the National Lending Library Unit.

In actually dealing with readers the assistant should never consider it sufficient to point to a section: he should himself take the reader to the shelves and see that he understands which books are likely to contain the information he needs. It is necessary at all times to remember the confusing impression which even the best organized library gives a reader when he first enters it, and to keep in mind that what is commonplace to the librarian may be completely strange and incomprehensible to the reader. Wherever possible, a reader should be asked as he leaves the library whether he has found the material he needed: very often such a question will bring the response that the reader has found only part of what he wants and thus give the assistant the opportunity to offer further help.

Every enquiry should be treated as important: few people take the trouble to enter a library and ask questions just to amuse themselves. The job of a librarian is to provide information without questioning to what purpose it may be put, or the circumstances which gave rise to the enquiry (apart from any light which this may throw on the subject). Some enquiries which at first sight appear to be futile, often turn out to be of great importance to the reader: thus, the reader who wanted pictures of animals playing musical instruments was discovered to be writing a serious work on the development of caricature. Furthermore, as a general rule, no assistant should ever be allowed to give his own personal opinion in answer to an enquiry: his duty is to give the answer from published information and not to guess more or less correctly what the answer may be. After all, the reader is capable of guessing for himself.

All unsatisfied enquiries should be noted and every effort taken afterwards to find out what are their correct answers. Very often the answering of a query long after its being made will be of academic interest only, since the reader may have found the solution from some other source or may have abandoned the search altogether, but the information thus obtained may still be of use to some other reader on another occasion. Moreover, it is good training for the librarian who thus gets into the habit of making every effort to find an answer to every enquiry. If the solution is obtained from some hitherto unsuspected source, the source should be noted in the information file (see page 120) and also pointed out to all members of the staff at the time. It is at this point that many first-class librarians fall down for they prefer to keep such information to themselves. No library assistant should attempt to establish a monopoly of being the only person capable of answering difficult reference enquiries. All knowledge of books and other libraries should be freely shared between all members of the staff, for the public look on the library as a whole and are not really concerned with which assistant answers their enquiries, any more than they ask the name of the postman who delivers their letters each day. Readers should be encouraged to know individual members of the staff by name and to ask for them if they wish to do so, but when they are acknowledging any help they may have received the assistant concerned should be careful to point out that it is the result of the co-operation of the staff as a whole. It is only in this way that a library of any kind can establish a reputation for good and efficient service.

The Vertical File

THE value of the vertical file in assisting the reader cannot be overestimated: it is the key to much topical and ephemeral, as well as much highly specialized, information which has not reached—and may never achieve—more permanent form. It is the bridge between the bookstock and the current periodical or newspaper. In it the librarian may hope to find the knowledge which supplements or corrects the latest edition of a yearbook and the last issue of a standard manual. In it the reader may often discover much material which, important though it may be, has not warranted detailed cataloguing, and would otherwise remain unnoticed. Properly planned and administered, the vertical file can earn the library many tributes which the book-stock alone could not elicit, but its planning and administration demand imagination and thorough treatment together with a larger proportion of the staff's time than most libraries can afford.

The vertical file usually consists of a nest of steel or wooden drawers of standard size capable of holding foolscap manila folders. But these are not essential: a competent vertical file can at a pinch be constructed from a miscellany of old boxes and envelopes: it is the contents, their arrangement and revision, which determine whether the vertical file is efficient or not. The foolscap-size steel drawer is however sufficiently universal to warrant the description given here.

There can be no hard-and-fast rule as to what is to be included in the vertical file. Material which in one library is considered worthy of being shelved with the bookstock may in another be relegated to the vertical file because the needs of that library differ from those of the other. Roughly speaking, however, it may be said that material which cannot stand up by itself on the ordinary shelves and which is not worth binding should be put in the vertical file—but only if it is worth retaining in the library's collection. Most pamphlet material is best put in the vertical file, for if it is included in the ordinary stock its lack of stiff covers quickly causes it to droop over the neighbouring books, to become tattered and to collect dust. For the more important pamphlet material it is possible to remedy this by attaching stiff covers or otherwise reinforcing it, but even so the inclusion of too many such items on the shelves tends to delay identification of individual items and to make the arrangement of stock more difficult.

The vertical file must not be considered at any time the proper place for material which would otherwise be thrown away. Items of this nature should never be put in the vertical file, for the contents quickly become suspect and neglected if they include much rubbish. Selection for the vertical file should be based on the same principles and should be just as severe as that for the ordinary bookstock, and the decision made to include any material in the vertical file only after it has been agreed that this location will exploit it best.

In addition to pamphlet material, news-clippings, charts, maps, plans, illustrations and samples can often be usefully included. Whenever any extended piece of research is carried out on behalf of a reader, or wherever a special bibliography is compiled, an extra carbon copy should be taken for inclusion under the appropriate heading in the vertical file. Additional material will be included according to the particular needs of the library.

If the vertical file is to be a success, it is necessary for it to be viewed as a whole, so that its contents relate to one another and form an integrated collection of sources. To achieve this it is necessary to put one assistant in charge of the file and to make him responsible for the selection, inclusion, arrangement, cataloguing and indexing of such items. The contents of the file—unlike those of the shelves which are specially designed to attract attention (sometimes far beyond their true worth)—remain

anonymous and indistinguishable one from another in their
manila folders, until the assistant introduces the contents of the
appropriate folder to the reader. But in order to do this it is
necessary to introduce a uniform system of subject headings
throughout the file, and to provide adequate indexes.

Many librarians believe that it is useless to keep anything in a
modern library which is not properly catalogued and classified.
It is true that items which are not so treated are very often overlooked when they are needed. The solution, though by no means
satisfactory, would appear to be a compromise in which everything possible is catalogued and classified and the remainder is
grouped under specific subject headings with a separate index of
the headings used. Those items which are classified and catalogued are really part of the bookstock, and their inclusion in the
vertical file is just a matter of convenience. Such items can be
filed, it will be found, in two parallel sequences in the standard
foolscap drawer, oversize items being placed spine upwards in
a separate sequence at the beginning or the end. If their classification numbers are boldly written in the top left-hand corner of
the front cover, they will be easier to find and replace here than
if they were kept on the shelves.

There will always remain at least a few items which are not
worth cataloguing or classification and yet must be retained in
the library for a short time. Such material will include information of forthcoming events, propaganda material of the more
substantial type, pre-prints and off-prints of topical interest,
extracts from books and periodicals which throw light on
problems which particularly interest readers but which are not
sufficiently authoritative to be used as more than incidental
information, etc. Each of these items should be awarded a
specific subject heading and placed in the folder bearing that
heading. A 5-inch by 3-inch catalogue card should be made for
the subject heading and filed, along with any necessary references, in the information file. Thus, whether there are two or
fifty items on this subject in the file, one subject card will represent them all. Whenever any material is inserted in the vertical

file, the contents of the folder should be inspected for material which has become superseded or out-of-date and can safely be withdrawn. This will ensure that the contents of the more popular folders will be frequently revised. It then remains to see that the contents of the less-used folders are also revised, and to ensure this a routine should be arranged by which the contents of the vertical file are completely revised once or twice during the course of the year. If at any time a folder is completely emptied, care should be taken to ensure that the subject heading and its references are removed from the information file.

Catalogued material should have its location in the vertical file entered on all catalogue cards relating to it, and withdrawal of these should follow the lines adopted for the withdrawal of books and other more permanent items.

There are three main systems of arrangement of vertical file material in current use: alphabetically by subject, numerically by classification number, and chronologically in order of addition to the library. Subject arrangement alphabetically is similar to the arrangement of the contents of an encyclopaedia and is well-suited to the needs of the average non-specialist reader, particularly if he is encouraged to use the vertical file by himself. The classified arrangement of folders has however the advantage of paralleling the classified arrangement of books on the shelves and, in the hands of a good assistant, can be made most satisfactory in satisfying the wants of readers. Chronological arrangement in the order of addition to the library is followed by some specialist libraries which base their files on the Kaiser system: this method relies on detailed indexing and requires the intermediary of the staff at all times for efficient service, so that its cost is beyond the budget of most libraries. Whatever the system of arrangement adopted, the main points to be observed are consistency and frequent revision of contents, without which the vertical file is likely to be of little use. Ideally, the vertical file collection should be kept close to the Readers' Adviser's desk where it can be exploited in connection with readers' enquiries.

The Illustrations Collection

ONE of the most useful additions to any library's resources is the illustrations collection. An illustration not only throws considerable light on the information contained in any printed description, but can also often explain more easily and more clearly a detail or an event than many hundreds of words. Illustration is a wide general term and can cover many different items in this particular context—photographs, drawings, paintings, portraits, engravings, slides, transparencies, etc.—and all of them can be put to good use in information work. Potential users of the material thus collected include many reference library readers, in addition to lecturers, teachers, journalists, display and exhibition designers, and local people of all kinds. Properly organized, the illustrations collection has unlimited possibilities for helping all sorts of enquirers and for extending the work of the library throughout the community it serves.

The material for an illustrations collection is comparatively easy to obtain and need cost very little. Pictures can be cut out of old magazines, newspapers and damaged books, used picture postcards can be collected, posters and other travel agents' hand-outs utilized, and so on—all is grist for this purpose, and once the collection has got under way, it is surprising how many readers will be willing to help from their own collections. In fact, there is usually an overwhelming amount of material available, and the librarian is therefore faced with the necessity for being selective if the collection is to prove of real value.

As a general principle it can be assumed that a comprehensive illustrations collection should comprise at least fifty thousand items before it can safely be deemed to be of use, and it is wise to avoid giving too much publicity to the collection in its early stages—a disappointed reader rarely returns. Nor can one illustration of a subject be regarded as sufficient: if it is a statue, views will be wanted from all sides, if a harbour is depicted, users may well need pictures showing the harbour at various stages in its history, if a portrait, then other pictures showing the subject at other points in his career may be necessary for various purposes. On the other hand, it is hardly necessary for the library to collect many illustrations showing almost the same view or aspect, unless special needs for duplicates (such as might be wanted for a study group) are likely to arise. It is not possible to lay down hard and fast rules: the librarian must be guided by the individual needs of his own readers.

There are various ways of filing illustrations: they can be stored in boxes, in file covers of various types, or loose in vertical or lateral files. The main essentials are that they should be well protected—from dust, damage, and mishandling—and that they should be easy to consult. Thus, even the method of arrangement must be varied to suit local needs: a specialized library may well adopt a classified arrangement which reflects the arrangement of its books and documents, while a public library may find that an alphabetical arrangement similar to that used in an encyclopaedia (with its divisions, cross-references, etc.) may be more suited to the requirements of the general public. In the latter case, the collection can be made self-indexing, and need have no other adjuncts, beyond a master-list of headings and references for the use and guidance of the organiser of the collection.

An illustrations collection, if it is to be of real value, must be a *living* collection to which additions and withdrawals are frequently made. A severe system of withdrawals is certainly necessary to keep the collection from taking up too much space and to ensure that everything retained is worth keeping. Thus, if a better colour reproduction of a painting is added, there is no need to keep the inferior copy; the addition of the original photograph of an event renders the half-tone copy clipped from a newspaper unnecessary. On the other hand, illustrations of recent events are always in great demand and can help the work of the library considerably: thus, for some little time press photographs of the Hovercraft in action were almost the only information which the average library could produce when that method of transport was first released for public demonstration.

Many libraries mount their illustrations on suitable backing sheets and much can be done in this way to make the collection more attractive, more easily handled and more useful: thus, variations in the colours of the backing sheets can be utilized to differentiate between various types of subject—views, people, events, inanimate objects, etc.—and thus aid both identification and filing processes. But in most libraries there is no need to back the great majority of illustrations—such protection(which may also include transparent cellophane envelopes, lamination, etc.), can safely be kept for those items which are irreplaceable. Most illustrations are expendable, and the work of preparing additions to the collection can be accelerated by reserving backing, etc., for the few items of real value.

Some items are asked for year after year—pictures of traditional Yuletide scenes, highwaymen, banquets, fairies, outerspace vehicles, etc., are in constant demand by commercial artists, scene designers, etc., and it is wise to keep such favourites out of the general collection and conveniently near at hand. The library's use of the collection for its own displays will help to discover any weaknesses in subject coverage.

Outside Resources

HOWEVER large the library there will be some questions and some needs which cannot be supplied from its own stock: the interests of readers are wider than the subject-content of any one library. Some of these queries cannot be answered from printed matter at all: they may concern information which has never been formulated, or they may be without any possible solution. But for the most part they are merely enquiries which are outside the scope of the individual library: their answers will probably be found in the appropriate special collections.

In order to find the answer to specialist enquiries it is necessary to have a good knowledge of library resources. In addition to the public libraries there are the university and college libraries, and the specialist collections of government departments, professional, trade and learned societies, industrial and commercial organizations, cathedrals and churches and private foundations, research associations and public corporations. The wealth of these libraries has never been fully recorded. ASLIB in Britain and the Special Libraries Association in the United States have both issued detailed directories of the specialist collections of their respective countries, but even so there is room for still more detailed analysis. Fortunately, in specific fields much has been done to show the resources on a single subject or group of subjects more fully and, in addition, the growing number of union lists of periodicals serve indirectly to indicate where further special material is likely to be found. In addition, the Bibliographical Centers in the United States and the National Central Library in Britain have further records of such material.

But these sources by themselves are not sufficient for the wants of the individual library. Each library has its local interests and needs. For instance, a public library will have special requirements in the field of the local history of its own area, and it will also have access to special collections and sources of information on the subject which are of no particular interest to any library outside that part of the country. In addition, most libraries have access to special collections—belonging to private persons or organizations—whose use is not generally extended further afield. Moreover, every library is in touch with at least one or two specialists whom it is able to approach occasionally for advice and help. All these sources, being mainly of local interest, are unrecorded elsewhere, and must be included in the desk information file if every assistant is to be aware and make effective use of them.

Contacts such as these are slowly built up over a period of many years and usually on a basis of mutual aid. It often happens that a specialist or industrial or commercial organization, in return for assistance rendered by the library, will place its expert knowledge and resources at the library's disposal. Such offers are genuine and must be used with the greatest care: no reader should be referred to such a source unless the library has first ascertained that he will be welcome and that the information he needs is available there. At the same time, private sources such as these should only be used when all others have failed, and then only if the reader is one who will not abuse them or queer the pitch for the next reader by a too casual acceptance of the facilities offered. Care should certainly be taken to follow up the results of any enquiry which has been referred elsewhere, to make suitable acknowledgment afterwards and to ensure that no misunderstanding has occurred.

During the past few years national systems of interlending material have become an everyday feature of library work on which librarians have come to rely with increasing confidence. This is one of the most valuable services which a library can offer a reader, and it is to the credit of British librarianship that it should have led the world in voluntarily establishing such a comprehensive and efficient system. It is also interesting to note that the Americans have developed such services through their Bibliographical Centers to still further lengths and that they have now taken the lead in recording and analysing the resources of many areas in the United States. Yet greater co-operation remains however to be developed on a regional level, and within groups of libraries concerned with the same subject-fields.

Thus libraries which normally co-operate with each other to the extent of interlending books could well follow the pioneer example of the medical and legal libraries by defining their subject interests, by transferring material outside these fields to more suitable libraries, and by establishing a policy of joint consultation over the purchase of more expensive items. In this way, money, staff and time may all be made available for other purposes. From this naturally follows such possibilities as the pooling of difficult enquiries, direct loans for urgent requests, the elimination of postage refunds after a trial period (the office work on this is usually out of all proportion to the small sums of money involved), the mutual notification of new additions, co-operative storage, and the standardisation of technique, forms and methods wherever they affect other libraries, as well as some exchange of staff for additional experience, etc. Again, many systems of inter-

79

lending do not fully cope with readers' needs in the fields of foreign publications, international organization and government documents, large reference works, some periodicals, and other essential items. Here too the solution probably lies within the regional or subject-group area rather than on a national level.

It is often the case that a reader wishes to obtain for his own use a copy of part of a book or of a periodical article. This can of course be copied out by hand, but in some cases—such as detailed statistics, illustrations, maps, etc.—the process of copying accurately is arduous, lengthy or impossible, and may keep the volume involved out of the hands of other readers for longer than is desirable. Here is a case where provision of one of the many cheap copying processes is warranted, and wherever possible the library should offer copies at as low as cost as possible. Where the library does not possess the necessary apparatus, arrangements can often be made for the copying to be done at a nearby library or by a local photographic firm. Moreover, where such a service can be offered, it eliminates the need for overmuch lending of scarce, valuable or much-used material. Care must of course be taken to avoid any infringement of copyright without permission.

A second service which should be offered is access to apparatus for reading microfilms and microcards. Where rare or valuable material cannot be borrowed, it is sometimes possible to obtain a microfilm or microcard which the reader can study at leisure if he has access to a suitable reader. Again, many libraries are buying microfilms and microcards of material or special interest to them. If the library can provide readers—apparatus at present still too expensive for the majority of students and research workers to buy for themselves—they will have increasing use and will greatly extend the range of the library's resources.

Tape and wire recorders are already much in use in research libraries and the larger public libraries. Most of these machines are run from batteries, but there seems no reason why the library should not allow a reader to plug in his machine to a suitable power outlet where necessary. Not every reader can however afford a recorder of this description, and the provision of coin-operated typewriters—such as is done in many American libraries—would seem a logical development for any library which wishes to give its readers the fullest possible assistance.

Making an Index

NEARLY every librarian has occasion to compile an index from time to time: it may be for a booklist or a bibliography, for a journal, for a local history, or for a set of trade catalogues. While training in cataloguing and classification is excellent preparation for this work, indexing remains a specialized art which must be studied separately if good indexes are to be produced. The main requirement of any index is that it should provide a ready reference to every item of value in a book, journal, etc., and none to unrewarding points. Thus, in the sentence: "The railway was eventually extended to include

lapsed before or during the war are being resumed. Some of these owe their new life to the generosity of <u>Unesco</u> whose work in this field cannot be overpraised. These newer items warrant careful study for many of them revise and correct the contents of the older bibliographies considerably. It is possible to keep in touch with the publication of new bibliographies by a regular search of the columns of the <u>*Times Literary Supplement*</u> which reviews most of the more general bibliographies, and by examining the entries under the appropriate subjects in the issues of the <u>*Bibliographical index*</u> which is the most comprehensive record of the present time. And to these, we now have the welcome addition of <u>Unesco's *Bibliography, documentation, terminology*</u> (Paris, 1961 to date), which has a truly international range.

Most libraries have, as part of their basic stock, a collection of the bibliographies of most use to them, and these are freely available to their members. In the search for particular bibliographies there is, moreover, a very useful union list (published by the Greater London Division of the Association of Assistant Librarians early in 1951) which shows the <u>whereabouts of copies of the more</u> important bibliographies in London's libraries. But it must be admitted that librarians give inadequate support to bibliographical effort, as the sales figures for such fine pieces of work as the <u>*Index translationum*</u> or <u>*Archivum*</u> unfortunately demonstrate.

It must be remembered too that there are *living* bibliographies: that

In the above material to be indexed, *Times Literary Supplement* would be given an entry 'BIBLIOGRAPHIES, reviews' and *whereabouts of copies* . . . 'BIBLIOGRAPHIES, location,'

Parton and Damside, but no service was provided on Sundays",
it is clear that reference to Railway Services, Parton, and Damside, must be included; it is a moot point however as to the value
of including any reference to Sunday railway services, unless this
question proves to be of some importance in the general context
of the work.

Before starting an index, it is essential to read through the
material thoroughly in page proof. On re-reading, words and
passages can be underlined in pencil and notes made of suitable
headings and references in the margins as on the previous page.

This preliminary survey is essential as indexers tend to give
varying degrees of emphasis to subjects and aspects of subjects,
until they are able to assess their relative importance throughout
the work.

The next stage is to make entries on separate slips or cards for
all items to be indexed; thus, some of the items above could be
entered as follows:

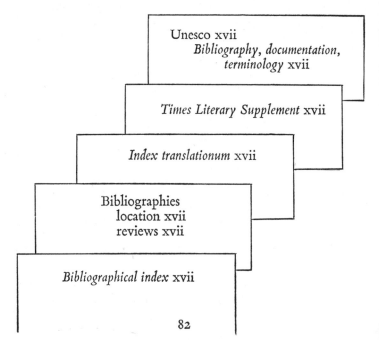

Unesco xvii
        Bibliography, documentation,
                terminology xvii

Times Literary Supplement xvii

Index translationum xvii

Bibliographies
    location xvii
    reviews xvii

Bibliographical index xvii

As the work proceeds, the indexer will discover that he often changes his mind about headings and references in accordance with the development of the subject: this is all to the good, since it shows that his appreciation of the needs of the users of the index—which are and must necessarily be paramount—is developing all the time. The only point to watch here is to ensure that the indexer alters his cross-references wherever necessary. Choice of names, subject headings, etc., should all conform as far as possible to the cataloguing practice in the individual library though different treatment which clearly benefits the reader should not be ruled out on the grounds of maintaining consistency with cataloguing practice.

When the index slips are completed they must be checked with the text for accuracy of page number references, and then sorted into alphabetical order. Then the editing beings: this comprises amalgamating entries for the same heading and breaking down large entries under sub-headings, aspects, etc.; checking for adequate cross-references and ensuring that all such references "lead somewhere" and do not produce the vicious circle which still appears too often in modern indexes; and for viewing the index as a whole and making certain that it is a consistent and a co-ordinated piece of work. This is the most important step in indexing and one which, owing to the speed with which most indexing must be done, is least satisfactorily performed. In checking the adequacy of references the principles of chain-indexing will be found to be of great assistance. The completed index is then typed double-spaced on quarto sheets and sent to the printers, and then follows through the normal stages of proof-reading.

The main points to watch are that the index is adequate within the space assigned to it, that it indexes subjects and ideas as well as personal and place names, and that it is comprehensive in the sense that it includes prefatory matter, appendices, illustrations, diagrams, etc., whenever they are informative and of value to the majority of possible readers. When the librarian is inexperienced in indexing, it is wise to try one's hand first at a short book which has already been well indexed: a comparison afterwards of one's own *independent* efforts with the printed index soon shows up one's weaknesses and errors. Within an individual index it is essential to maintain consistency in such points as alphabetization, use of the singular or plural form of subject-headings, use of the popular or scientific forms of subject-headings, and the breaking-down into aspects, etc., of any entry comprising references to more than five or so different passages (long lists of numbers are frustrating to the reader and tend to make the index less used than it should be). As part of general assistance to readers, the well-made index to, for example, a local journal or to the Council proceedings, can prove of great importance.

Compiling a Bibliography

MOST librarians are called upon to compile a bibliography or reading list of a subject from time to time, but in many cases at such infrequent intervals that they must consider the whole task anew on each occasion. The danger in this is that they may omit one or more steps in the process of ensuring that their bibliography is of sufficient coverage to satisfy the needs of the reader.

The main essential is to proceed carefully in all cases from the general to the particular, even though some of the stages may, after consideration, be rejected as inapplicable to the individual subject under treatment. Thus, supporting material such as maps and statistics would usually not be needed in the case of the majority of literary topics, while thematic catalogues and catalogues raisonnés would be irrelevant in the documentation of technological or scientific material.

Nevertheless, it is possible to outline the main features that should be considered in compiling bibliographies. The following headings, arranged in logical order of consideration, will be found of general application.

		Examples
Bibliographies:	(a) general	Besterman's World Bibliography of bibliographies
	(b) particular	The US Department of Agriculture's Bibliography of agriculture
Guides to the literature of a subject		Park and Whitford's Physics literature
Lists of periodicals		Ulrich's Periodicals directory
Library catalogues		Royal Institute of British Architects' Catalogue
Abstracts and indexes		Cumulative indexes to journals and groups of journals, such as the US Atomic Commission's Nuclear science abstracts, or The Engineering index
Dictionaries and encyclopaedias		
	(a) general	Encyclopaedia Britannica
	(b) special	Kirk and Othmer's Encyclopedia of Chemical Technology
Handbooks and yearbooks		Kempe's Engineer's year book
Statistics		Registrar-General's Statistical review of England and Wales
Textbooks		Gray's Anatomy
Popular outlines		Hogben's Science for the citizen
Monographs		Archer Taylor's Book catalogues
Government and international organization documents		Public general acts Bank of International Settlement's publications
Standards and Patents		Publications of the British Standards Institution, and the International Standards Organization

History		Lockhart's The fall of the Safavi dynasty
Periodical articles	(a) general	Lancet
	(b) special	Biological bulletin
Non-book materials		Maps, gramophone records, tapes, films, films strips, illustrations, etc.
Review sources and services		British medical bulletin Subscription books bulletin
Sources of information		Other libraries, other organizations, specialists and experts, editorial departments of journals, etc.

To each entry it is well to append an annotation indicating the scope (and, where necessary, the arrangement) of relevant material, *e.g.*:

Margary, Ivan D. Roman roads in Britain: vol. II. North of the Foss Way—Bristol Channel (including Wales and Scotland). Phoenix House, 1957. 288 p. illus. maps. Includes short bibliographies for each item.

Where the bibliography is large, or when its contents are complicated, it is helpful to add a contents-list of section headings, and also an index of subjects and aspects of subjects and, if possible, of authors and significant titles. In any case, an introductory note should explain that the bibliography is naturally selective and that further references will be found in the items mentioned under the heading Bibliographies. It should also be indicated what items are available immediately and which must be obtained from other libraries and under what conditions. A cover-title with the name and address and telephone number (and extension) of the Library and its Reference Department should be included, and the bibliography should always bear the date of compilation.

File copies of such bibliographies should always be kept in the information file: they form an excellent basis for future work and enquiry providing that the limitation of their date and selective nature are always borne in mind.

*Introduction to Library Service for Children

IN any scheme for introducing young people to their public library service, a librarian should begin by seeking the co-operation of the local education authority. He will then be brought into touch with all the schools in the area, and the visits can take place during school hours. The instruction in the library should, of course, be entirely in the hands of the library staff. The best time for a class visit is when the boys and girls are approaching 15 and the end of school-days is in sight, though younger children have been known to get great profit and pleasure from the experience. Not more than twenty pupils should attend in a group and, if only one visit is possible, it should last at least for an hour and three quarters.

The tendency of any adult in front of a class of young people is to tell them too much. If the librarian can make clear, first, that the library is free and available to all; next, that many books may be borrowed for home reading but that others are always to be found in the library; that the books are arranged on a plan which can be followed in the catalogue; and lastly, that some books are prepared especially to give information quickly—then a very good foundation will have been laid. Most young people learn more by doing than by listening and it is therefore important to keep the spoken instruction as brief and concise as possible and to follow it with exercises which bring into use the principles which have been explained.

With regard to practical work it should be noted first, that every exercise should be carefully prepared and checked before

* This chapter has been written and contributed, by kind permission of Mr John Bebbington, City Librarian and Information Officer of Sheffield, by Miss P. E. Charlesworth, Organizer of School Instruction Classes in the Sheffield City Libraries.

the class arrives; that, since some pupils will quickly outstrip others, plenty of reserve material should be ready; and finally, that the visit will run more smoothly if the questions—printed or typed—are set out so as to allow spaces for the answers to be written on the question paper itself.

About forty minutes may be spent in the Lending Library. The chief points to be explained are: the division between fiction and non-fiction; the arrangement of the books by their subjects; the use of numbers to indicate the various subjects; the subject entries in the catalogue; and, how a particular book can be traced from the catalogue to its place on the shelves. Practical exercises will have to be adapted to suit each particular catalogue but the essential purpose must be to show that it acts as an index to the shelves. And one exercise at least should give the author and title of a book which has to be looked up in the catalogue and then sought on the shelves. To allow a fair chance of success, a marked duplicate copy of each book to be found should be placed on the shelves before the class arrives.

In the Reference Library it is wise to limit the instruction—with one exception—to the quick-reference book which is constructed on a single alphabetical sequence. The exception is the local directory, which should be shown to the class, and the chief sections indicated. Boys and girls are always alive to the value and interest of such a detailed record of their own surroundings. The quick-reference books which can suitably be introduced to an average class and on which practical exercises can be based include dictionaries, encyclopaedias (general and special), dictionaries of biography, and gazetteers. A note suggesting specific titles can be found at the end of this chapter. Some of the books will already be familiar to pupils, but the librarian must try to present them not as individual books but rather as a collection of tools for obtaining precise information.

In setting questions to be answered from reference works it is best to keep to the kind which admits of only one correct answer. The young reader has then a single clear objective, and the librarian can see at a glance whether that objective has been gained. It is well, too, to grade the questions on some such scale as these:

First Stage calling simply for the use of an alphabetical sequence and two pieces of straightforward deduction, *e.g.*
In the *Encyclopaedia Britannica*, volume 8, find "ermine"
    (a) What colour is the winter coat of the ermine?
    (b) How long is its tail?
In *Chamber's Encyclopaedia*, volume 5, find "Elba"
    (a) What is the area of this island?
    (b) What three fruit trees flourish here?

Second Stage testing knowledge of the sources of information, but requiring only a minimum deduction, *e.g.*
In what year did Christopher Columbus, the discoverer of America, die?
What is the full name of Lord Nuffield, a well-known living industrialist?
In what city was Beethoven, the great composer of music, born?
What articles of food are made in the town of Melton Mowbray?
What colour is meant by the word "cerulean"?
Who wrote a story called "Kim"?

Third Stage testing knowledge of sources again but calling for rather more reading and, perhaps, reference to more than one source, *e.g.*
In what city was Handel's "Messiah" performed for the first time? Which English king was present at the first London performance?
Who was the second man to swim the English Channel? Who was the first woman to do so?

To attempt more than this, to consider—for instance—methods of study or to assess one work of reference in comparison with another will almost certainly prove too ambitious. In any group of young people who have worked through the three stages suggested there will assuredly be some interested enough to come back to the Reference Library to make further explorations for themselves.

In Sheffield, a scheme based on the principles outlined in this chapter but with some difference of detail, has been in operation continuously since 1942. It is administered by the Education and Libraries Joint Sub-Committee and all types of school participate, the pupils attending in their third year as seniors (*i.e.*, at 13-14). The large Central Library building allows classes of forty to attend at one time, the two groups of twenty each being supervised by a member of the Library's staff. A separate lesson, followed by practical exercises, is given on the Directories, so that while one group is engaged with the quick-reference books, the other is working first in the Lending Library and then with the Directories, the two groups changing over after about an hour. As so many classes attend it is worth while to print the basic questions (*i.e.*, those which cover the minimum effort in each department). For each of the forty different question papers an answer paper (or "key") is given to the teacher who accompanies the class. This is not an essential, but it allows each pupil to mark his own work and can form a useful basis for a revision lesson when the class has returned to school.

A note on reference books for classes of pupils aged 13-15

The class should, of course, see the Reference Library and form some impression of its extent, but it is a great advantage, from a practical point of view, if a collection of reference books can be set aside solely for the use of classes:

Dictionaries

The collection should include perhaps one dictionary compiled especially for younger readers (*e.g.*, the *Thorndike junior dictionary*) for the sake of the less advanced pupils, but the majority of the class can be expected to use an ordinary single-volume dictionary of adult standard.

Encyclopaedias

There should be at least one encyclopaedia in many volumes (*e.g.*, the *Encyclopaedia Britannica* or *Chambers's Encyclopaedia*), and several of the single-volume encyclopaedias, *Hutchinson's Twentieth Century encyclopaedia* and Collins' *New age encyclopaedia* being particularly suitable. The *Oxford junior encyclopaedia*, though it offers excellent reading, is not well adapted to class work as the Index volume to the twelve separate sequences is of necessity too constantly in demand.

Other quick-reference works which may be recommended for class use include:

Chambers's Biographical dictionary
Webster's Biographical dictionary
Chambers's Dictionary of scientists
Who's who
Chambers's World gazetteer and geographical dictionary
Bartholomew's Survey gazetteer of the British Isles
The Oxford dictionary of English Christian names
A Dictionary of abbreviations
The Science reader's companion; edited by G. E. Speck
The Encyclopaedia of painting; edited by Bernard Myers
The Oxford companion to English literature
The Oxford companion to American literature
The Oxford companion to music
Grove's Dictionary of music and musicians (even an early
    edition of this work is still a most serviceable tool)

With the development of further education in this country there is likely to be more demand for instruction in the use of books and libraries for young students, particularly for those following a vocational course.

For the majority, the Reference Library will be the most obvious choice. Here again, the tendency may well be to offer more than the inexperienced student can assimilate, and it is a wise policy to keep to a comparatively small collection of books; to emphasise the importance of such essential but frequently ignored features as the table of contents, the index and the table of abbreviations; and to set straightforward questions that can be answered briefly. A tour of the whole library building can be made the basis for surveying the library service as a whole. For this purpose Sheffield is fortunate in possessing a coloured film, "Books in hand"* which, in the space of some twenty minutes, reviews every facet of the library service: the public departments, administration, the branch and junior libraries and extension activities; thus supplementing and revising what has been learnt in the course of a visit. The film has been found valuable, too, in stimulating the interest of young people in Youth Clubs and similar institutions.

A more informal and very attractive method of encouraging children in the use of books and libraries is the organization of a Book Week, usually in close collaboration with the National Book League, publishers and authors of children's books, and local booksellers. Features which are usually included in such events comprise a series of lectures covering various subjects (Hornsey's choice of Careers as a theme was especially successful, since each guest-lecturer was notable in his or her field); correlated displays of books; displays on how to use books and libraries (including the classification and the catalogues); displays on printing, paper-making, book-binding, etc.; displays of illustrations drawn from the Illustrations Collection; displays of quick-reference works; film shows of items about books and libraries; various competitions, quizzes, brains trusts, etc., to ensure that the children are able to play an active part in the Book Week. As in all activities with children, it is essential when planning a Book Week to maintain the closest contact with the education authorities, the staff of the schools, and social and

---

* This is a 16mm. sound film, with commentary by Mr. Alvar Liddell. It is available free to any organisation with a good projector and a trained operator. Copies can also be purchased at £42 each.

welfare workers who come into contact with children through clubs, etc., especially in the early stages when experts such as these can have a hand in deciding what will be most suitable and can help to give the scheme adequate publicity.

The whole question of the possibilities of Book Weeks and Library Weeks is treated in detail and with great interest in Mr Harold Jolliffe's *Public Library Extension Activities* (The Library Association, 1962).

Name..

CITY OF SHEFFIELD
EDUCATION AND LIBRARIES, ART GALLERIES
AND MUSEUMS JOINT SUB-COMMITTEE

LIBRARY VISIT

Remember, if you cannot find what you want, the staff will always help you.

ANSWER THESE QUESTIONS IN THE LENDING LIBRARY:

1. What is the number for books about Watch repairing?...............................

2. Find in the catalogue the card for this book: "The Face of the earth" by J. H. CURLE. Write the number here (a).....................Then look for this book on the shelves. (b) What is the title of Chapter I?

   ....

ANSWER THESE QUESTIONS IN THE SCIENCE AND COMMERCE LIBRARY:

3. Find a directory of Gloucester. (54)

   (a) What is the name of the inn at 5 Cambridge Street, Gloucester?

   ....

   (b) Find the address of Mrs Gladys Ayliffe, tobacconist, in Gloucester.

   ....

ANSWER THESE QUESTIONS IN THE COMMITTEE ROOM:

4. In the *Encyclopaedia Britannica*, volume 17, find "Patience".

   (a) What is another name for this game?...

   (b) How many varieties are there?...

5. (a) What is the full name of Viscount Nuffield, a famous living industrialist?

   ....

   (b) Write on the line below the name of the book in which you found the answer ....

94

Paper No. 17.

CITY OF SHEFFIELD
EDUCATION AND LIBRARIES, ART GALLERIES
AND MUSEUMS JOINT SUB-COMMITTEE

———

LIBRARY VISIT

———

KEY

———

1. 681.114.

2. (*a*) 910.1
    (*b*) By land and water.

3. (*a*) Locomotive Inn.
    (*b*) 102 Southgate Street.

4. (*a*) Solitaire.
    (*b*) Two.

5. (*a*) William Richard Morris.
    (*b*) Any of the following:
        Who's Who
        The International Who's Who

        Chambers's Encyclopaedia, volume 10
        Hutchinson's Twentieth Century Encyclopaedia
        Nelson's Encyclopaedia
        Collins New Age Encyclopedia

        Webster's Biographical Dictionary

NOTE: The *Nuttall Encyclopaedia* gives only William Morris, Viscount Nuffield.

Some easier examples of Stage 2

14.

Name...

EXTRA PAPERS

1. The EMU is a kind of *bird*. In what country is he found?

    ....

2. BILLINGSGATE is the name of a *market*. What is sold there?

    ....

3. POLO is a *game*:

    How many people form a team in polo?...................................

    What animal takes part in this game?.....................................

4. CHESS is a *game*:

    How many people play in a game of chess?...............................

    How many squares are there on a chess board?...........................

KEY

1. Australia.   14.

2. Fish.

3. Four.   A horse.

4. Two.   Sixty-four.

SHEFFIELD CITY LIBRARIES   5.

GRAMMAR SCHOOLS

Name...

1. VENEZUELA is a republic in South America.
    What does the name mean?

    ....

    What is the capital of Venezuela?

    ....

2. How many masts has a BRIG?

    ....

3. Fred ARCHER (1857-86) was famous in one sport. What was it?

    ....

4. What is the name of the National Anthem of Belgium?

    ....

    Who composed it?

    ....

KEY

1. Little Venice.   G.S.5.
    Carácas.

2. Two.

3. Horse-racing.

4. La Brabançonne.
    Campenhout (Dechez).

Question 4 is an example of Stage 3

97

Name ....

CITY OF SHEFFIELD
EDUCATION AND LIBRARIES, ART GALLERIES
AND MUSEUMS JOINT SUB-COMMITTEE

LIBRARY VISIT

Remember, if you cannot find what you want, the staff will always help you.

ANSWER THESE QUESTIONS IN THE LENDING LIBRARY:

1. What is the number for books about Toadstools? ....

2. Find in the catalogue the card for this book: "Alexander the Great" by B. I. WHEELER. Write the number here (a) ....Then

look for this book on the shelves. (b) What is the title of chapter I?............

....

ANSWER THESE QUESTIONS IN THE SCIENCE AND COMMERCE LIBRARY:

3. Find a directory of Southampton. (110)

(a) What is the name of the hotel at 1 Padwell Road, Southampton?

....

(b) What is the address of Tongs and Son, basket makers, in Southampton?

....

ANSWER THESE QUESTIONS IN THE COMMITTEE ROOM:

4. In the *Encyclopædia Britannica*, volume 4, find "Buzzard".

(a) What shape is the head of the buzzard? ....

(b) How many species of buzzard are there in the British Isles? ....

5. (a) In what year was Florence Nightingale born? (She died in 1910).

....

(b) Write on the line below the name of the book in which you found the answer.

....

Specimen of an actual question paper

Library Lectures

THE institution of regular introductory lectures in the use of books and libraries is rarely found outside the largest public libraries. Usually the lack of sufficient staff prevents the addition of such facilities as this to an already full routine. Yet those who are familiar with the work of museums and art galleries will have noticed how popular are well-organized tours of introduction under the guidance of a qualified and experienced lecturer. In a similar fashion, there is much scope for lectures on the use of books and libraries even in the smallest systems, but only if each lecture is well planned and competently carried out.

Many libraries are too crowded and too busy to allow of such lectures being given during the time that they are open for normal use, but such lectures could be planned to take place after hours. Few people like to listen to a talk on books without any form of illustration, and a lecture on the use of libraries could well be backed up by displays of selected material in each of the departments visited. If the lecture is made peripatetic—that is, if the audience are taken from department to department and shown well-arranged displays of outstanding material belonging to each part of the library, and if each department is described by its librarian-in-charge—the variety of surroundings and speakers will add to the interest and success of the visit.

Lectures such as these are best given to small groups of people, and admission to the lectures should be controlled by the issue of tickets or individual invitations so that there will not be too many readers at any one lecture. In each department chairs should be arranged to allow the audience to sit while listening to a description of its work and functions, and an opportunity should then be given for the visitors to inspect the displays put out for their inspection, and to ask questions in as informal manner as possible.

Small libraries may well shirk this type of activity, pleading that they have not the resources necessary to provide really interesting and attractive displays. But the rarer and more expensive material can often be borrowed from larger libraries near by, or through such organizations as the National Book League. In the same way, guest speakers can often be found among one's colleagues in the same region and, in fact, a little ingenuity will soon produce a programme which is both valuable and inviting.

For example, a lecture is to be given on the use of books and libraries in a small provincial public library comprising lending, reference, junior and periodicals departments. The meeting starts off in the most attractive department on the ground floor—usually the children's library. Here the audience is welcomed by the Chairman of the libraries committee or the Librarian who says a few words explaining the way libraries are run, what they cost the individual citizen, and what he can reasonably expect in return for his money. This introductory talk is given in an atmosphere of the utmost informality and, to achieve this, comfortable chairs are arranged in a semicircle in a corner of the room around the speaker, who himself increases the informality of the occasion by remaining seated while he is addressing his audience.

After this, the Children's Librarian follows with a brief talk on the importance of children's learning to use books early in life, and a description of the work of her department, including such features as story hours and school libraries. Arranged in the room is a good display of outstanding children's books in good editions, interspersed perhaps with examples of children's painting, handicrafts, etc.

The visitors then move to the Lending Library where they are shown a little of the mechanics of the issue and discharge of books, and where they hear what steps are taken to produce any particular work for which a reader may ask, including the resources of interlibrary loans. The opportunity is here seized to hand out copies of any booklists, guides to the library, and other recently-published aids to readers. Prominently displayed are topical selections of books and periodical articles on subjects much in the public eye.

The party then goes to the Periodicals Room where the periodicals are displayed without their covers and are grouped under subjects. Nearby is shown a selection of periodicals' indexes—both British and American—and microfilm and microcard readers (both fitted with material ready for showing) are strategically placed so that the audience can fully appreciate what remarkable possibilities are now within the reach of even isolated students and research workers.

In the Reference Library the Reference Librarian then emphasizes the importance of periodicals in supplying information which has not yet (and may never attain) book form, and demonstrates how knowledge of new subjects is discovered from newspaper and periodicals' indexes. Displays in this department may include a history of printing showing both early and modern examples of fine craftsmanship, a few specimens of the results of the misuse of books, and a selection of local history material including famous archives, maps, prints, works of local authors, etc.

In addition to the examples given here, there are many other features which might be incorporated according to the nature of the district in which the library is situated, and according to contemporary local and national events. Thus, the formation or popularity of amateur dramatic societies would warrant a display of relevant material backed up by period costumes, pictures of famous actors and models of different kinds of theatres, stage machinery, etc. New industries could be represented by periodicals and books devoted to these trades, supported by examples of the types of articles manufactured. National and international events would play their part as they do in any other form of publicity. In addition, there are several films and strip-films about libraries and books which can add considerably to the attraction of the proceedings.* The main point is to ensure that the complete tour is not too long—certainly not more than 70 or 80

---

* Details of current available items can be obtained from the Librarian and Information Officer of the Library Association, Chaucer House, Malet Place, London, W.C.1.

minutes—and that everything goes with a swing which, of course, means careful rehearsal and timing. Members of the staff should be introduced by name, and readers should be encouraged to seek their advice and help more fully when they use the library. Since there will always be one or two people in the audience who are not members of the library, it is well to make provision not only to allow them to join but also to borrow a book as they leave the building.

Many modifications are naturally necessary before this type of introductory tour can be applied to special libraries, but the basic principles remain the same—that is, the provision of an opportunity for the librarian and the reader to meet each other in a less formal and hurried atmosphere. Some of the larger organizations have an ingenious system by which interested people are invited to come to hear a talk given in the library by a guest speaker—usually someone prominent in library or information work. Though the address may be devoted to the industry rather than more specifically to sources of information, the indirect approach has the effect of arousing interest in the latter which can be intensified and maintained by displays, demonstrations, etc., related to topical subjects.

Part IV

REFERENCE MATERIAL

Maps and Gazetteers

THERE are few libraries which do not possess at least a small collection of maps and gazetteers: they are a very necessary part of any library even though they are not always exploited as fully as they should be. Part of the difficulty of ensuring their full use lies in the problems of their size and storage: these are administrative points which have no place here,* but their exploitation is an essential part of service to readers. Fortunately there are very few library assistants who do not fall readily under the spell of maps once they are given any work with them, and the more members of the staff who are or have been connected with their care and use the better from the point of view of assistance to readers.

There are many kinds of maps, all of which have their place in various types of libraries. First of all, there are the maps of the locality in which the library is situate: a general library should possess all the maps it can obtain which depict the town itself and the immediately surrounding area. These may include town plans, development schemes, historical maps, Ordnance Survey maps of scales ranging from 1 inch to fifty inches to the mile, street maps from directories, public utility maps, civil defence maps, electoral and administrative maps, and many more which feature various aspects of the life of the community. Larger libraries will extend such a collection to include maps on similar subjects for the whole county or region, so that readers will be assured of as complete coverage as possible for all the districts within easy reach of the library.

Libraries of all kinds need maps covering the whole country: these are of many different kinds—physical, political, economic, communications, geological, land utilization, social surveys, etc., mostly in comparatively small scales, and sometimes—as in the

* Fully covered in *The storage and conservation of maps*, Royal Geographical Society, 1955.

case of geological and land utilization surveys—accompanied by memoirs and descriptive matter in book and pamphlet form. For those areas in which the library is particularly interested the library will buy larger scale maps, just as the library which is concerned with a particular subject will acquire all the maps it can obtain in that field. Since the war most counties and large towns have published development schemes containing many valuable maps especially drawn for that purpose. These maps include a wealth of information which if not unobtainable elsewhere would certainly be difficult to discover. To buy copies of these schemes is one of the cheapest and best ways of providing up-to-date information on social and industrial and economic affairs.

In addition, all libraries have other large map resources in the form of maps and plans which are included in books, such as encyclopaedias which usually provide maps and sketch plans of the chief places they describe, directories, and many books and pamphlets on travel, history and geography, economics and politics. To these must be added such general atlases as the library possesses—such as *The Times Survey Atlas*, the *Rand McNally Commercial Atlas*, the Touring Club Italiano's *Atlante Internazionale*, and Stieler's pre-war *Hand-Atlas*—any atlases of special subjects, and the more comprehensive guide books. Maps, in fact, are to be found in many places: for instance, Ayer's *Directory of Newspapers and Periodicals* includes a map of every state in North America, and some of the telephone directories—such as those issued in New Zealand—include excellent town plans.

To support the map collection it is essential to have a number of gazetteers. For general world purposes there are the *Columbia Lippincott Gazetteer*, *Webster's Geographical Dictionary*, and the indexes to the larger atlases such as *The Times*, the *Britannica*, and to such large encyclopaedias as the *Enciclopedia Italiana*. These however are only sufficient for preliminary identification of a place, and to make certain that there is no ambiguity it is essential to provide national gazetteers such as those issued by the British

Ordnance Survey, the United States Navy, the Permanent Committee on Geographical Names, and other authoritative bodies. Additional material of a gazetteer nature can be obtained from guide books such as the Baedeker and Blue Guide series, the magnificent American Guide series, and those issued in particular localities.

To exploit maps to the full it is wise to use as many pictorial devices as possible. Thus, to most important series of maps indexes are published separately: these can be mounted on card, marked with those maps the library possesses, and shown to readers so that they can indicate the map they need by identifying the inclusive region. Where individual index maps are not available, it is sometimes possible to achieve the equivalent by providing a copy of the general map catalogue of the survey body: while this does not always contain index maps, it will give a list of the maps available, and sometimes give brief annotations. Lists of new issues of these catalogues are included every year in the *Bibliographie Cartographique Internationale*.

To ensure the fullest exploitation of maps, it is essential that they be adequately classified and listed, and stored in such a form that it is easy to find them and to replace them accurately. Good lighting, space to examine them, and staff who are completely familiar with the system of arranging them, will enable the readers to make thorough use of one of the most attractive and useful features of the modern library.

Directories and Annuals

THE basis of all good reference work is the expert exploitation of a well-selected collection of yearbooks and directories It. is not sufficient merely to have a good collection of annuals: in order to make effective use of them it is necessary to ensure that all members of the staff are familiar with their contents and individual method of arrangement. Moreover, an expert staff cannot give the best service if the annuals and directories are badly selected. It is the combination of good book selection and good research work which forms the best basis for good reference service.

In these days the number of annuals and directories is overwhelming, and it is by no means easy to select the best, once the first hundred or so basic items have been ordered. Most subjects are represented by at least two annuals which overlap to a great extent in the information they provide. An outstanding example of this is the number of directories concerned with the papermaking trades which are now being published. Since no library is able to buy annuals without stint—without detrimental effect on the funds available for the rest of the bookstock—it is necessary to select very carefully the annual which best represents its subject from the point of view of the readers using that particular library. Thus, for instance, in choosing a nautical almanac the librarian has the choice of at least three well-established publications, specimen copies of which he must examine with care before deciding which he means to buy. As in the case of the selection of periodicals, it is unwise to experiment too widely in their purchase, for readers get used to a particular periodical or annual—whether it be good or bad—and the information it offers, and they do not readily appreciate the substitution of a similar work with whose slightly different method of arrangement and contents they have to make themselves familiar.

During the post-war period libraries have received news of many new annuals, some of them covering new fields, and others attempting to supersede the standard publications on popular subjects. It is a great temptation to subscribe to many of these, but any extension of the list of annuals taken must be based on a preliminary survey of the field already covered. Before another annual is added on a subject already well represented, it should first be considered whether there are any subjects not yet covered which are of particular interest to the locality or subject-fields of the individual library. This is a problem which is more easily solved in the provinces (where local industries and interests are usually more clearly defined) than in London in the case of public libraries, but to the special library it is not likely to present any great difficulty.

Once therefore it has been decided which subjects must be represented and which annuals are to cover them, standing orders must be placed to ensure that new editions are received as soon as they are published. Care should be taken to secure suitable editions: for instance *Whitaker's Almanack* is published in three editions, one of which is an abridged version lacking the last three hundred pages of the complete issue. Other annuals are published in special library editions as well as in bound and unbound paper-covered editions: cloth-bound copies should always be bought wherever heavy use is likely, or where previous editions are filed permanently for reference. A record should be kept of all annuals, containing details of price, source of supply, supplements, and date when the new edition is expected to be ready.

Not all annuals are purchased: some very valuable items—such as the yearbooks of learned societies and of professional, commercial and industrial organizations—are often presented to the library. They are none the less valuable for that, and are usually well worth filing for at least a few years. Gifts such as these, however, are less easy to keep track of, since their publication is sometimes recorded (if at all) some weeks after issue, and copies are sometimes distributed to libraries well after they have been issued to members. Thus the situation can arise where a reader will complain that the library still has last year's issue on the shelves when he has positively seen a copy of the new edition in private hands.

It is not possible to file the previous issues of all annuals received, but the most valuable should certainly be kept as long as there is space to hold them. What are the most important items naturally varies with the individual interests of the library and also—to a certain extent—with what files are available in neighbouring libraries and organizations. By careful co-operation with nearby libraries it is possible to make a very large number of back files available within a radius of a few miles, without any one library's devoting a disproportionate amount of stackspace to annuals. Although much of the information in the previous editions of yearbooks may be out-of-date, or may have been printed afresh in the current issues, there often remains information which, for example, may be of great use in tracing the career of an important person, the history of the development of a process or of a firm, or the illustrations and working details of a piece of outmoded equipment. These files contain much material which is of use in establishing details of the social history of the period they represent, and even their advertisements can often yield useful material on such subjects as fashion, retail prices, etc., which research workers will need in the future.

Those who have visited the Guildhall Library in London will have noticed in the excellent Commercial Library that each annual has a notice pasted on its cover saying that it is the current issue, and that a new edition may be expected on such-and-such a date. This is very helpful to the reader, and might well be extended to read something like this:

> This is the current edition. A new edition is published about (May) each year. Previous editions, dating from the year (1902) are available on application.

in which the bracketed items would vary with the individual annual. The catalogue entries should also contain information concerning any previous issues on file and any special shelf-marks.

The shelf-mark is of especial importance, for it is usual to shelve the most used annuals outside the main classification sequence and at a point conveniently near to the entrance to the library or to the reference or commercial department. Where this is done, it is a good practice to shelve them in alphabetical order by the significant word in the title, and to give them a running number to assist readers in finding them and in replacing them quickly and accurately. Some libraries group their yearbooks roughly by subject and then number them in sequence. These two methods seem to be appreciated by readers more than an arrangement in classified order either separately on in the general sequence of books. Nearby should be displayed a dictionary index of the titles and subjects of the annuals, so that readers can discover the yearbooks they want without difficulty.

Some annuals are published as part of the subscription to the corresponding technical journal: the *Pottery Gazette Yearbook* and the *Electrical Trades Directory* (the "blue book" of the *Electrical Journal*) are good examples. In such cases, libraries may sometimes find it difficult or impossible to secure a copy of the yearbook without subscribing to the periodical. Where both periodical and annual are taken, the cover of both periodical and yearbook should each bear a notice drawing attention to the other, since the periodical is to some extent a supplement to its yearbook —and vice versa.

Once an annual has been received and recorded it should be carefully examined. If it is a new edition of one already taken, it should be studied for the addition of any new material and the elimination of any standard features, and for any alterations in arrangement or emphasis. Much of this information can usually be discovered from the preface. If the yearbook is new to the library it should be studied most carefully, for each annual has its own system of arrangement, abbreviations, symbols and eccentricities, and until these have been mastered it cannot be fully exploited. Whether new or old, the contents list and the index should be examined for material whose inclusion cannot necessarily be expected from the annual's title and may not be recorded under a familiar heading. Thus, who would confidently expect the *Catholic Directory* to say where a Chinese-speaking person can confess in his own language in England, or the *Official Yearbook of the Church of England* to give detailed information on Queen Anne's Bounty? Whatever unusual features are discovered should be indexed by subject in the Reference Desk information file (see pages 64 and 70), which all assistants in the department should be required to glance through regularly for new additions and alterations. A special watch should be kept for supplements, lists of addenda and errata, and loose insets, and a system maintained by which none of these is ever overlooked when the yearbook is being used.

If the library is large enough to be able to subscribe to more than one copy of some of the more important annuals—or where small quick-reference collections are maintained at branch libraries— it is well to keep on file two copies of the edition immediately previous to the current one. Libraries often receive requests for the loan of back numbers of annuals, and the filing of a second copy will enable these loans to be made without detriment to the interests of readers who rely on the library to keep on file a complete set for reference.

Many of the more reputable annuals now contain bibliographies: the *Statesman's Year-Book*, the *Yearbook of Education*, and *Trusts and Foundations*, are only some of the many examples which will immediately spring to mind. These bibliographies repay checking with the catalogue for they often record uncommercial or privately-printed documents which may not be listed elsewhere.

The value of telephone directories is not always fully realized: the classified sections of some of the foreign telephone directories are sometimes of far more value to libraries than the commercial directories of the countries concerned, for the latter so often appear unreliable or incomplete and are usually very expensive. In the same way, the *Post Offices of the United Kingdom* is as good and as up-to-date a gazetteer of Britain as anyone could desire for general purposes.

But the chief value of annuals lies in the fact that they are the result of years of experience and experiment. The aim of each compiler of a successful yearbook has been to provide his reader with all the information which he can reasonably expect to find inside its covers. Crammed into odd corners are a thousand and one facts and pieces of curious or essential knowledge. With the aid of a little patience and a good memory, the outstanding items in each yearbook can be noted and used to good advantage. Any onlooker who cares to stand at a busy reference desk and listen for a little while to the enquiries will be surprised to see how many queries are solved from a comparatively small group of essential annuals. How many more then could probably be solved just as quickly had the contents of the remaining annuals been known to the staff just as thoroughly? So much in fact of the success of the work of a reference librarian depends on his knowing what lies between the covers of his most popular books.

SOME ESSENTIAL ANNUALS

GENERAL
Annual Register
International Who's Who
Whitaker's Almanack
Who's Who
World Almanac

ARMED FORCES
Air Force List
Army List
Navy List

BOOKS AND PERIODICALS
Government Publications Consolidated (Annual) List
* Library Association's British Humanities Index
Newspaper Press Directory
* Willing's Press Guide
Writer's and Artist's Year Book
* British National Bibliography

COMMERCE
Directory of Directors
FBI Register of British Manufacturers
Kelly's Directory of Merchants, Manufacturers and Shippers

---

* *Willing's* and the *British Humanities Index* have quarterly supplements; the *British National Bibliography* is published weekly, and has frequent cumulations as well as an annual volume.

Kelly's Post Office Directory of London
Post Office Guide
Sell's Registered Telegraphic Addresses
Stock Exchange Official Year Book
Telephone Directories (both alphabetical and classified)

MEDICINE
Dentist's Register
Hospitals' Year Book
Medical Directory (rather than the Register, which gives less
    "background" information)

POLITICS, ADMINISTRATION AND ECONOMICS
Central Office of Information's Britain: an official handbook
Municipal Year Book
Post Offices of the United Kingdom
R.A.C. or A.A. Year Book
Statesman's Year-Book

SHIPPING
Lloyd's Calendar
Nautical Almanac

SOCIOLOGY
Annual Charities Register
Crockford's Clerical Directory
Debrett's or Burke's Peerage
Kelly's Handbook to the Titled, Landed and Official Classes
Law List
Official Rules of Sports and Games
Stone's Justices Manual
Yearbook of the United Nations
Yearbook of the Universities of the Commonwealth

STATISTICS
Board of Trade Annual Statement of the Trade of the United
    Kingdom
Central Statistical Office's Annual Abstract of Statistics
Registrar-General's Statistical Review of England and Wales

TECHNOLOGY
* Library Association's British Technology Index
  Kempe's Engineer's Year Book
  Laxton's and Lockwood's Builders' Price Book
  Library Association Yearbook

and, *Current British Directories* (which has such a useful subject-index to annuals and their main contents), and the voters' or electoral roll as well as the local directory, and current national and local public transport timetables.

Encyclopaedias and Biographical Reference Works

ENCYCLOPAEDIAS provide the basis of any enquiry work since they not only give a summary of the information on the subject up to the date when that particular entry was revised, but they often include short bibliographies—in the case of the greater works such as the *Enciclopedia Italiana* both these items are usually extensive and the references to sources of information cover material in many languages. The encyclopaedia therefore serves to put the enquirer on the right lines for conducting his research, but there are certain considerations which he must keep in mind if the encyclopaedia is to be of full use to him.

In the first place, it is essential to discover the system of arrangement. Most encyclopaedias are nowadays arranged by alphabetical order of subject, though the *Oxford Junior Encyclopaedia* and the Dutch *ENSIE* are grouped by large subject fields. But even within the alphabetical system of arrangement there are variations: the *Encyclopaedia Britannica* and the *Encyclopaedia Americana*, for instance, tend to commission long articles on a subject and all its ramifications, while *Larousse*, the *Brockhaus* and the *Winkler Prins* follow the system of short entries on specific subjects. A brief test of the treatment of subjects known to the reader will soon serve to show which method is followed. There is also the question of the state of revision: some encyclopaedias,

* Monthly, cumulating annually.

such as *Chambers's* and again the *Brockhaus,* have a clear system of numbered editions, each new edition denoting a thorough revision of contents. In the case, however, of the *Americana* and the *Britannica,* new issues are published very frequently and there is a process of continuous revision by which a certain proportion of the contents are revised each year, the encyclopaedia being completely revised every ten years or so. In the latter case, unless the editions are compared page by page, it is sometimes difficult to ascertain how recently an individual article has been revised. Most librarians would welcome the dating of articles in encyclopaedias which follow the principle of continuous revision.

There are other features which are well worth examining, such as the inclusion of illustrations and maps, the system of indexing and references, the provision of appendices and yearbooks, the inclusion of gazetteers and map references, the general date of statistical material quoted, the signing of articles, the general scope as stated in the Preface and any evidence of bias or special policy. Encyclopaedias never go wholly out of date and old editions are well worth keeping since they often include articles on subjects no longer treated in current reference books.

Encyclopaedias are especially important for the biographical information they contain, and often they are the only sources of information on minor figures as far as the average library is concerned. The more important countries however have their own national dictionaries of biography—Britain, the United States, Australia and New Zealand are among those who have, while South Africa and Canada are without such valuable aids, and France and Germany are only very slowly supplementing their old biographical dictionaries with new works. To these national biographical dictionaries must be added any revisions and corrections: the Institute of Historical Research, for instance, publishes frequent emendations to the *Dictionary of National Biography* in its *Bulletin.* Then there are the current biographical reference works, such as the national who's whos, peerages, directories of officials, biographical dictionaries of various professional and commercial and industrial groups, university and college registers, school lists, family histories, and other items. In addition to these there are various international works such as *World Biography*, the *International Who's Who*, and the invaluable H. W. Wilson publications *Current Biography* and the *Biography Index*. More than one country publishes cumulations of its past who's whos in the form of multi-annual who was whos, but these do not entirely take the place of the original volumes and should be treated as a partial index to their contents. Almost all historical works—especially those dealing with the history of individual institutions and organizations such as schools, regiments, associations and societies, movements, etc., include much valuable biographical material and are part of the biographical resources of the library, whether it be general or specialist.

Official Publications

OFFICIAL publications—that is, the publications of local and national governments, and those issued by international bodies, etc.—are not as fully used in the average library as they deserve. This is partly due to the fact that they are rarely reviewed or even noticed in the press, and that they are usually unbound so that they do not often appear on the open shelves. They often have additional disadvantages such as the lack of a memorable title, some ambiguity over actual authorship, and other such points which render them difficult to find in any author catalogue. They are in fact dependent on careful subject cataloguing for their full exploitation, and this they do not always receive. Thus much important statistical and other information on current topics lies neglected in many a library owing to its appearance in the form of an official publication.

The most valuable source of statistical information for almost any library is the vast series of publications issued by its own national government: the publications of departments dealing with such subjects as trade, agriculture, customs and excise, labour, etc., are particularly useful here, while those of many other departments such as education, overseas territories, health, etc., may also include important historical and sociological information. In addition, governments are publishers of maps and plans, guides, museum and art gallery catalogues, public records of former times, official diplomatic and trade documents throwing much light on the history of the country, and numerous practical leaflets on such subjects as crops, machinery, accident and fire prevention, etc.

The publications of international bodies such as the United Nations and its agencies—World Health Organization, Food and Agriculture Organization, Unesco, etc.—the International Labour Office, the International Court of Justice, etc., are of increasing importance as the files grow and comparable statistical and other information becomes available for a number of years. Especially useful are the statistical abstracts and the surveys of the problems of a particular problem either generally or in relation to individual countries. Thus the Bank for International Reconstruction has issued a number of valuable reports on the social and economic structure of some of the less developed countries which provide information not easily found elsewhere.

Similarly, the publications of state and city governments can be of more than local interest: the items issued by such authorities as the London County Council and such States as California and New York in the U.S.A. are evidence of this. There is also a multiplicity of material issued officially or semi-officially by universities, trade and professional organizations, research associations, trusts and funds, societies and groups, which are of paramount importance to any library which caters for the serious reader. To discover most of these it is essential to study the national bibliographies, the announcements in the more scholarly journals, and the columns of the *Vertical File Index* and *Public Affairs Information Service Bulletin*, in addition to the official lists of publications issued by the more important governments. And it is well to keep a note of the approximate dates on which new editions of frequently-revised material are due.

Local Collections

THERE are very few public libraries which have not formed some kind of local collection, and this in many cases has been very carefully built up and catalogued so that it rivals in its comprehension and organization the best special collections in other subjects. This is as it should be, for the local collection is one of the most valuable aids to readers and has a far wider appeal than any other section of the library. The fact that it relates to the immediate locality makes it unique, and the prerequisite of local knowledge gives the librarian and his staff the opportunity of demonstrating what can be achieved by the application of modern bibliographical methods to the documentation of a specific subject.

The scope of the modern local collection is considerable: not only does it include printed material (books, periodicals, pamphlets, etc.) on the history, topography and antiquities of the area, but it will also include ecclesiastical surveys and history, directories and guides, the genealogy and histories of local families, and biographies of local worthies. In addition, there will be both new and old prints, maps, plans and charts of the neighbourhood, and there will be collections of portraits, posters, notices, playbills, programmes, tradesmen's cards, tokens, and any other printed material relating to local events of any period.

Such items are however of minor importance compared with the archive material which is the backbone of any good local collection. It is from the archive material that the printed works have largely drawn their facts and statistics, and it follows that the vast majority of the archives will be in manuscript form. These will include material relating to the administration of the district, such as charters, deeds, ratebooks, manorial and other court books, poll books, voters' registers, etc. They will also include the records of local societies and associations and institutions, as well as those of local business firms. Finally, they may well include the records of local families where the individual family or some of its members have played any prominent part in the history or development of the area.

Some libraries also make a point of including books which have been locally printed or published, and those which—while having no local reference in their subject matter—have been written by local authors. This type of material can be valuable from time to time, but its place as an intrinsic part of the average local collection has yet to be established. Mr John L. Hobbs's *Local History and the Library* (Deutsch, 1962), in a comprehensive survey of the whole subject, treats the whole of this topic in considerable detail.

Abstracts and Indexes

PERIODICAL articles play an increasingly important part in information work to-day, and the full exploitation of periodicals is one of the most important problems which faces the librarian in any type of library. The advance of knowledge is in fact so swift that books are often partly out of date before they are printed. The extent of knowledge in any field consists then of the information given in the books on the subject *plus* the periodical articles that have been published since the latest book was written. If every periodical article was thoroughly indexed so that it could be discovered by subject approach there would be no very great difficulty in providing accurate information on most subjects. It is unfortunate that the position at the moment is not as straightforward as this, and that there are few signs of any great improvements in the near future.

There are few countries that publish indexes to their periodicals, and there is none which covers all the journals issued in its territory. The United States is the most advanced in the indexing of its periodicals: thanks to the H. W. Wilson Company there are two general indexes—the *Reader's Guide to Periodical Literature* and the *International Index*—and a number of more specialized indexes such as the *Bibliographic Index*, the *Education Index*, the *Art Index*, etc. In addition, there are two independent indexes:

the *Engineering Index* (which includes brief summaries of the articles) and the magnificent *Public Affairs Information Service Bulletin*. All these are published at frequent intervals and are cumulated into annual and, in most cases, multi-annual volumes.

In Britain there are the Library Association's *British Humanities Index* and *British Technology Index*, each of which cumulates annually; and Canada, Australia and South Africa all have indexes to their more important periodicals. Sweden, Germany, Spain and a number of other European countries have good periodical indexes but, in common with the USA and Britain, not one of these completely covers the national output of serials.

It is fortunate that in many professions and industries there is additional help available in the shape of indexes and abstracts covering, usually on an international basis, a large subject field. *Chemical Abstracts*, *Fuel Abstracts*, *Social Science Abstracts*, the *Index Medicus*, and *Library Literature*, together with the invaluable *Applied Science and Technology Index*, are among the many titles that immediately spring to mind in this connection. The standards vary of course very much: thus, some abstracts include thesis literature as well as periodical articles, some are written by the authors themselves and others by professional abstractors, some are issued by professional bodies and others by commercial agencies, some omit items in foreign languages, and some avoid overlapping with other services. Of late there has been a tendency to try to eliminate duplication of effort and thus to find space for extending the field covered, but even so much material remains unindexed. Thus it is possible, for instance, for important articles to appear in such fugitive media as house journals and newsletters—items not often included in the standard indexes.

Most libraries therefore find it necessary, wherever they are attempting to cover a specific subject field thoroughly, to construct their own indexes of material not included in the standard indexes, and also to make temporary index entries for important topical items until they appear in the latter. To ensure adequate assistance to readers it is therefore important to see that all periodical indexes relating to the subjects in which the library is interested are taken, and then to make a survey of those periodicals which are not indexed and decide which should be covered by the library's own index. In doing so, it is well worth adding entries for periodicals not taken by the library if they are available in some nearby library to which readers are likely to be able to obtain access: and this in turn may involve the creation of a joint scheme with neighbouring libraries with the same interests by which as large a number of periodicals as possible is subscribed, and any unnecessary duplication of the less important items is eliminated. Such a scheme will naturally embrace such points as the loan and copying of periodical articles, the exchange of index entries, and the retention and binding of past issues.

Catalogues and Bibliographies

THE smaller the library the more necessary it is to have a good selection of the catalogues of other libraries and of the chief bibliographies. This would appear to be somewhat paradoxical at first sight for, when there is little money for the purchase of books, it would seem foolish to spend much of that fund on lists of books which the library does not possess. To take such an attitude is however parochial and unworthy of the present age, for it stems from the narrow viewpoint that the individual library is the only source of information for its readers. In these days of rapid travel and of highly-developed library co-operation no library is the sole resource for its members, and the provision of catalogues and bibliographies will help the reader both to identify the material which he feels is most likely to be of use to him and will also aid him in obtaining it. The identification of material is in fact one of the essential tasks of readers' advisory work and must be done first before any attempt is made to tap outside sources.

There are several important catalogues which should be part of the stock of all but the most specialized libraries: these include the three great national catalogues—those of the British Museum, the Bibliothèque Nationale, and the Library of Congress—and the London Library catalogue and the joint effort based principally on the collections of the London School of Economics which is known as the *London Bibliography of the Social Sciences.*

Specialist bibliographies are also of the greatest importance since they are based on expert knowledge of particular fields of information and often record items listed nowhere else. They have the additional advantage of frequent supplements in many cases. The following list includes the principal bibliographies and catalogues in the main subject fields, and many more specialized are listed each year in the *Bibliographic Index* published by the H. W. Wilson Company:

PHILOSOPHY AND THEOLOGY

Rand. Bibliography of Philosophy, Psychology and Cognate Subjects. 2 volumes. 1905 (reprinted 1949)

Bibliographie de la Philosophie, 1937 to date

Psychological Abstracts, 1927 to date

L'Année Psychologique, 1894 to date

Dr Williams's Library. Author Catalogues, 1841 to date

British and Foreign Bible Society. Historical Catalogue. 2 volumes in 4. 1903-11

Répertoire Général de Sciences Religieuses: Bibliographie. 1950 to date

Index to Religious Periodical Literature, 1949 to date

SOCIOLOGY

A London Bibliography of the Social Sciences, 1931-32 to date

Public Affairs Information Service Bulletin, 1951 to date

Bulletin Analytique de Documentation Politique, Économique et Sociale Contemporaine, 1946 to date

International Bibliography of Sociology, 1951 to date

International Bibliography of Political Science, 1953 to date

International Political Science Abstracts, 1951 to date

Foreign Affairs Bibliography, 1919 to date

International Bibliography of Economics, 1952 to date

Where to Look for Your Law. 14th edition. 1962
Index to Legal Periodicals, 1908 to date
A Legal Bibliography of the British Commonwealth of
   Nations. 2nd edition. 1955 to date
Education Index, 1929 to date
British Education Index, 1954 to date
Education Abstracts, 1949 to date
National Union of Teachers. Library Catalogue, 1959 to date

SCIENCE AND TECHNOLOGY
Science Museum Library, London. Bibliographies
New York Public Library. New Technical Books, 1915 to date
Technical Book Review Index, 1917 to date
Aslib Book List, 1935 to date
British Technology Index, 1962 to date
Applied Science and Technology Index, 1958 to date
Mathematical Reviews, 1940 to date
Chemical Abstracts, 1907 to date
Biological Abstracts, 1926 to date
Botanisches Zentralblatt, 1880-1919, 1922 to date
British Museum (Natural History). Catalogue, 1903 to date
Zoological Record, 1864 to date
Index Kewensis, 1893 to date
Nomenclator Zoologicus, 1939 to date
Catalogue of Lewis's Medical, Scientific and Technical Lend-
   ing Library, 1957 to date
Science Abstracts, 1897 to date
Index Medicus, 1960 to date
Engineering Index, 1884 to date
Index Aeronauticus, 1944 to date
Agricultural Index, 1916 to date
Bibliography of Agriculture, 1941 to date
International Institute of Agriculture. Catalogue. 1948
Royal Horticultural Society. The Lindley Library Catalogue.
   1927

FINE ARTS

Chamberlin. Guide to Art Reference Books. 1959
Art Index, 1929 to date
Bibliography of the History of British Art, 1934 to date
Royal Institute of British Architects. Catalogue. 2 volumes. 1937
Hiler. Bibliography of Costume. 1939
ALA Portrait Index. 1906
Monro. Index to Reproductions of European paintings. 1956
Photographic Abstracts, 1921 to date
British Catalogue of Music, 1957 to date
Loewenberg. Annals of the Opera. 2nd edition. 2 volumes. 1955
Sears. Song Index. 1926 (Supplement 1934)
Clough and Cuming. World's Encyclopaedia of Recorded Music, 1952 to date
Greenfield. Stereo Record Guide, 1960 to date
Library of Congress. Motion Pictures, 1894 to date

LANGUAGE AND LITERATURE

Index Translationum, 1932 to date
Linguistic Bibliography, 1939 to date
Cross. Bibliographical Guide to English Studies. Latest edition
Sequels. Latest edition
Cumulated Fiction Index. 1961
Fiction Catalog, 1960 to date
The Year's Work in Modern Language Studies, 1929 to date
The Cambridge Bibliography of English literature. 1940 to date
Annals of English literature, 1475 to 1950. 2nd edition. 1961
The Year's Work in English Studies, 1919 to date
Annual Bibliography of English Language and Literature, 1920 to date
Granger. Index to Poetry and Recitations. Revised edition. 1962
The Player's Library. 1950 to date

Firkins. Index of Plays, 1927 to date

Samuel French Ltd. Guide to Selecting Plays. Latest edition

Logasa and Ver Nooy. An Index to One-act Plays, 1924 to date

Short Story Index, 1953 to date

The Essay and General Literature Index, 1900 to date

Körner. Bibliographisches Handbuch des deutschen Schrifttums. Latest edition

Lanson. Manuel Bibliographique de la Littérature Française moderne, 1500-1900. New edition. 1921

Cabeen. A Critical Bibliography of French Literature. 7 volumes. 1947 to date

Talvart and Place. Bibliographie des Auteurs Modernes de Langue Française, 1928 to date

Nairn's Classical Handlist. 4th edition. 1960

L'Année Philologique, 1924 to date

Seymour Smith. The Classics in Translation. 1930

GEOGRAPHY, HISTORY AND BIOGRAPHY

Wright and Platt. Aids to Geographical Research. 1947

Cox. Reference Guide to the Literature of Travel, 1935 to date

Bibliographie Cartographique Internationale, 1936 to date

Bibliographie Géographique Internationale, 1891 to date

A Guide to Historical Literature. New edition. 1961

Helps for the Student of History, 1950 to date

Hyamson. Dictionary of Universal Biography. Latest edition

International Bibliography of Historical Sciences, 1926 to date

Annual Bulletin of Historical Literature, 1911 to date

Bibliography of British History, 1928 to date

Riches. Analytical Bibliography of Collective Biography. 1934

Biography Index, 1946 to date

Current Biography, 1940 to date

Royal Commonwealth Society. Subject Catalogue. 5 volumes. 1930-61

Whitmore. A Genealogical Guide. 1953
Gardner and Smith. Genealogical Research in England and
Wales. 2 volumes. 1956-59

Conclusion

THE work of assisting the reader is largely a matter of
commonsense coupled with a detailed and comprehensive
knowledge of books and human affairs. It is a kind of social
service and attracts many librarians who see in it a means of
putting to good use the experience they have gained from a life-
long study of printed material. It is unfortunate that it rarely
offers a career with prospects as good as those which are to be
found in the administrative branches of librarianship. In fact, for
many librarians the work of assistance to readers must remain a
short stage only in their progress towards deputy and chief
positions. For those however who are able to find posts in advisory work which are sufficiently well paid to enable them to
continue indefinitely in this branch of librarianship there is the
guarantee of a life whose interests are infinitely varied and
stimulating and one in which the satisfaction to be gained from
helping others is always present.

The best kind of training for advisory work is undoubtedly
that which gives the assistant considerable experience in as many
different branches of librarianship as possible before he embarks
on the task of assisting readers. Thus an assistant who has spent
some time in classifying and cataloguing books, in carrying out
the general routine processes in both central and branch libraries,
and who has had some experience in special or university as well
as public library work comes to the job of advising readers with
that flexibility of mind and understanding of the resources
available which are so essential to successful work. In addition,
experience in some field outside librarianship—teaching, commerce, industry, or the retail trades—gives additional breadth of
outlook in dealing with readers who are neither librarians nor
bookmen. Finally, a readers' adviser should have his examinations

behind him: if he has some part of his training still to do and some examinations still to take, he will not be free to use some of his leisure time in the wide reading and in taking part in outside activities which a good readers' adviser will almost automatically undertake. Perhaps it is best not to decide too soon on a career as readers' adviser or reference librarian, but rather to choose librarianship in general and to study from the inside the many different careers it now offers before finally making up one's mind. In the United States there is a much closer link between libraries and bookshops than in Britain: American librarians and booksellers have much the same training and see their problems from much the same angle. In the work of advising readers they recognize that the same problems face both types of bookmen. The situation is no different in Britain and, in the work of advising readers, much could be done to institute common courses of training which would fit assistants for both types of work and thus enlarge what is at the moment a rather limited field with few financial rewards.

Straightforward as assistance to readers usually is, it is remarkable how often people come away from their library unsatisfied or even with somewhat misleading or out-of-date information. Part of the fault lies in the understaffing of essential departments: even now, there are reference libraries in this country which are unsupervised, and there are special libraries in the charge of office clerks. The parsimonious attitude of the town council which haggles over suitable school buildings and attractive parks is reflected in out-of-date poorly furnished libraries and ill-stocked shelves. The same firm which will spend thousands of pounds on publicity will make do with last year's directory and thus send expensive samples to the wrong addresses. The same type of attitude is responsible too for the untrained staff which tries to cope with difficult queries, and for the overworked librarian who endeavours to do many kinds of work with one pair of hands.

The essential requirements of a library are two, and they are interdependent: books and librarians. A first-class collection of printed material is essential, but it does not become a library until it is in the capable hands of experienced librarians. Only then do the full resources of this material become available to the great majority of its readers. On the other hand, a well-trained body of librarians is wasted if the collection of books is inadequate. It is true, however, to say that a well-trained librarian can do more with a small well-chosen bookstock than an unskilled librarian can do with one many times larger. But in order to do so the librarian and his staff must not be hampered by too much routine work—a situation which is bound to occur if the staff is too small to cope with everyday routine.

In most libraries to-day it is unfortunately true that the librarian and his staff are overworked and that the routine is seriously hampering the work of their libraries. Where this is the case, the routine should be so arranged that the readers' adviser is left as free as possible of any duties outside his own particular job. This may mean cutting down routine duties in general, but there is still room for considerable pruning in the amount of records maintained by many libraries, and a survey of the present-day necessity for each individual process will certainly repay the time spent on it.

The work of assistance to readers is not one which will ever produce large statistics, if it is properly carried out. It is a job which requires much detail and patient thought and attention. Such work will not show much increase in statistical values year after year, but its worth can perhaps be measured to some extent by the letters of appreciation, the offers of reciprocal help and the gifts of books and other material which good advisory work earns from time to time.

Such work properly carried out allows little time for analysis, and yet the results of such study are invaluable. Wherever possible, simple records should be maintained of the types of questions, the time taken in handling them, and their success or failure —where enquiry forms are used (see pages 59 and 67) the material is already available and needs only simple analysis. These should be carefully studied to discover where the stock may usefully be extended to answer such questions and requirements in the future, and what outside sources have been discovered to hold valuable material which may be used on other occasions. Such analysis is more usually conducted only in the readers' adviser's head long after the day's work is finished, but this will mean that by reason of the many succeeding events much that was of importance has been forgotten meanwhile.

Most librarians who have taken part in the work of advising their readers will have come to the conclusion that most of their readers' needs have an answer somewhere in their own or their neighbours' libraries. The difficulty so far has been to find out where this information is to be found, and secondly to discover this source quickly enough for the purpose for which the reader wants it. At the moment, while it is fairly easy to track down a copy of any generally well-known book, or to find a book on any fairly popular subject, the machinery for tracing the rare book and the obscure subject remains cumbersome. The national system of interloan always supplies an answer to a library's request for such books or subjects but, as every librarian knows to his cost, sometimes long after the reader has obtained the information he requires from another source. The latest edition of the *ASLIB Directory* and the subject-index of the 1954-55 edition of the *Libraries, Art Galleries and Museums Year Book** give much guidance to those seeking information on specialist collections, but there still remains the need for further detailed analysis of resources such as various specialist groups are carrying out in their own fields. Secondly, it is necessary to make a nation-wide effort to persuade the many fine specialist libraries who remain outside the national interloan scheme to come into it and strengthen this remarkable system by making their resources available to research in general. This would apply also to those public libraries that have not recorded their reference library stocks in the regional catalogues. Only when these two objects have been achieved will it be possible to give what should be an everyday service in Britain: that is, a definite answer within

---

* New edition in preparation.

three days as to whether any particular book, pamphlet or periodical is available anywhere in the British Isles.

Again, there are some parts of the country where no great library service is available within fifty or a hundred miles or more. Here is a case where one of the county library headquarters or regional branches or one of the larger public library services should be specially developed by co-operation to meet such a need. In these days, even when no great space is at hand for expansion, it is possible to provide all the resources represented by the entries in Winchell in a comparatively small area by means of microfilm and microcards. When this kind of development is seriously undertaken it will at last be feasible to provide what is the right of every citizen—direct access to a library service embracing every type of library in the country and worthy of the times in which we live.

A Short Reading Course

THIS is one of the most fascinating subjects in the whole of librarianship, and it is well worth reading more extensively on the various aspects of assistance to readers in the vast amount of professional literature now available. Most of the newest ideas and suggestions first appear in the professional periodicals, and the several journals each print a number of features and original articles which help to keep one abreast of the current trends of thought and policy.

The *Assistant Librarian* will always be dearest to the hearts of all British librarians who have ever spent part of their early working years doing the routine and humdrum jobs which a junior assistant must undertake while he learns the fundamentals of librarianship. A glance through the long file of this periodical—covering some sixty years or more—will show the development of modern ideas in the profession, for the articles therein embody many of the pioneer suggestions of assistants who have since become leaders in the profession. Though the journal has had its lean periods it is remarkable for its persistence in publicizing ideas which were only quite slowly accepted by librarianship and in giving a chance to the younger librarians to voice their opinions. Since it embodies the more enthusiastic trends of librarianship, those who take the trouble to explore past issues and to keep an eye on its current numbers cannot fail to gain many good ideas which can be put to good use in assisting readers.

In addition to the many important and authoritative articles on this subject which appear in the *Library Association Record*, special attention should be paid to that journal's regular features on municipal, county, university and special library developments which are full of helpful hints on publicity and work with readers. Mr J. F. W. Bryon's monthly column "Off the record" in the *Librarian and Book World* is perhaps one of the most stimulating contributions to modern library journalism and helps to keep the librarian up to date with recent developments and modern practice. Similarly, the very careful summaries of Annual Reports extending back over many years in the *Library World* faithfully convey the answers found by many libraries to the problems which affect most systems. The *Library Review*, on the other hand, makes a distinctive contribution to librarianship in its humanistic approach and its close attention to literature, and often features articles from the point of view of the reader and the layman. Its columns have included contributions from most of the great names in librarianship, and a refreshingly international outlook has been maintained in its interests and coverage.

In the United States the most useful periodical from the point of view of this book is the *Wilson Library Bulletin* which has the great advantage of being very well illustrated, and very often gives clear photographs of displays and exhibitions, together with detailed descriptions of the "bright ideas" of readers' advisers. The *ALA Bulletin* gives many hints on current gadgets and techniques, and the *Library Journal* is also full of information on new inventions and professional trends, and again is especially valuable for its illustrations—a feature which is unfortunately almost non-existent in British professional literature.

In recent years much important material has been appearing in regional and house journals, such as the *London Librarian* and *Pharos* (the excellent "house organ" of the County Library system of Lanarkshire in Scotland) in Britain, and the *California Librarian* and the *Pioneer* (lavishly illustrated journal of Remington Rand) in the United States. These periodicals are well worth scanning for they have a less formal approach and give free play to new ideas and developments.

The best way to keep up to date with the wealth of information appearing in periodical form is to read regularly the Library Association's invaluable *Library Science Abstracts*, which makes an international survey of professional developments and activity in an evaluative fashion which ensures that the interested reader misses nothing of importance. Nor should the comprehensive H. W. Wilson Company's index *Library Literature* be overlooked: each article listed is given a short resumé if it is of sufficient importance (apart from easily accessible literature in the English language), and a glance through its columns in each quarterly issue will soon determine which items are of interest to the librarian. Other articles in *Special Libraries*, *College and Research Libraries*, *Library Quarterly*, and the *Stechert-Hafner Book News* provide from time to time very useful information for librarians engaged in information and readers' advisory work. Items in the more general periodicals are listed under the appropriate subject-headings in the *Reader's Guide to Periodical Literature*, the *International Index*, the *British Humanities Index*, *British Technology Index*, *Public Affairs Information Service Bulletin*, and even in the *Engineering Index* and the *Applied Science and Technology Index*. With such careful indexing available nowadays, sources for new ideas and inspiration are always at hand.

But the librarian should not stop here: many libraries are sufficiently public-spirited to circulate freely their annual reports and bulletins to other systems. Each item received should be carefully examined, ideas noted, and the material itself filed away for future reference. A good collection of library publicity material of this kind is a living textbook of librarianship which is more up to date and thorough than the best textbooks can possibly be. Here too are to be found photographs, diagrams and illustrations which never reach all the members of the profession who would be interested in them.

Among the few books on the subject, mention must be made of Philip Hepworth's *Assistance to Readers* (2nd edition, *Association of Assistant Librarians*, 1956; new edition in preparation) which is a thorough summary of readers' advisory work from the point of view of the Library Association's examination in this field; and D. J. Foskett's *Assistance to Readers in Lending Libraries* (James Clarke, 1952) which is based on practical experience in one of East London's best branch libraries, and his *Information Service in Libraries* (Crosby Lockwood, 1958), which covers a much wider field in a stimulating fashion.

This is headed a short reading course, but there is one point which must be added if the best advantage is to be made of the reading recommended. That is, that as many visits as possible should be paid to other libraries of all kinds and to the professional meetings held under the auspices of the various professional associations. The interchange of ideas is the lifeblood of the profession, and no librarian can visit a library—whether it be good or bad—or take part in a professional meeting, without learning something which will later stand him in good stead.

Index

Abstracts, 119-21
Adolescent libraries, 16, 22
Adolescents
  instruction in use of libraries, 22,
    23, 87-98
Advisory work with readers, 54-102
Aids to readers, xv-xviii, 28-52
ALA bulletin, 131
Annotations, 40-44
  author, 41
  catalogue entries, 42
  current interests, 42
  examples, 40-41
  local interests, 42
  special subjects, 42-3
Annuals and directories, 106-14
  contents, 111
  editions, 108-9
  essential items, 112-14
  filing, 108-9
  gifts, 108
  publication dates, 109
  selection, 107-8
  shelf marks, 109
  standing orders, 108
  subscription items, 110
Archives, 118-19
Art annotations, 43
Aslib, 29, 78
Assistance to readers, xv-xviii,
  54-102
Assistant librarian, 130-131
Association of Assistant Librarians,
  37, 133

Bebbington, J., vii, 87
Bibliographical centers, American,
  78, 79
Bibliographies, 121-26
  compilation, 84-7
  English-language publications, 28,
    29
  library catalogues, 30, 121-22

Bibliographies—*cont.*
  official documents, 28, 31
  pamphlet bibliographies, 29-30
  periodicals indexes, 30-31, 119-21
  special subjects, 29, 31, 122-26
  subject indexes, 29
Biographical reference works, 115-
  16
Birmingham public libraries, 38
Book jackets, 18
Book plates, 39
Book Weeks, 92-3
Booklists, Library, 34-8
  local, 37-8
  national, 37
  policy, 35-6
Booksellers and librarians, 127
Bookstack guiding, 7-8, 22
Bradford, S. C., xviii
Breaking of sequence, 11
Bristol public libraries, 38
British Museum publications, 29, 32,
  121
Bryon, J. F. W., 131
Bulletins, Library, 34-8
  contents, 35
  national, 37
  policy, 35-6
Business libraries, 16
By-laws, 39-40, 45

California University, Los Angeles,
  34
California librarian, 132
Carrels, 11
Catalogue guides, 23-5
Catalogues, 23-5
  published, 30, 38, 121-22
Charlesworth, Miss P. E., vii, 87
Charts, 72, 104-6
Children
  Book Weeks, 92-3

135

Royal Institute of British Architects
library publications, 29, 30

Samples, 72
Science annotations, 43
Scientific libraries, 69
Sequence of books, 11
Serials, 11-12, 14-15
indexes, 14
Sheffield city libraries, 38, 87-98
Shelf guiding, 7-9, 22
Shera, Jesse H., xviii
Shop window publicity, 47
Signs, 2-4
external, 3-4
internal, 5-6
position, 6
Size of books, 11
Sociology annotations, 42-3
Special libraries, 77-80
Special libraries, 132
Special Libraries Association, 78
Specialist enquiries, 77-80, 129-30
Spine titles, 9
Staff
information bureaux, 13
lectures and talks, 47-8
Stechert-Hafner book news, 132
Stevenson, W. B., v-vi, vii, 58
Street notices, 3-4, 46
Students, Training of, 87-98
Subject indexes, 22
Subject lists, Library, 35-6
Subject specialization, 79-80

Tape recorders, 80-81
Technical libraries, 16
Technology annotations, 43

Telephone directories, 111
publicity, 46
reference value, 111
Theology annotations, 42
Titles, spine, 9
Tours of library
adults, 99-102
children, 87-98
Training of students, 87-98
Typewriters, 81

Use of libraries, 2, 21-2
published guides, 21-2, 24-5, 32-4
training
adults, 99-102
children, 22, 23, 87-98

Vertical file, 71-4
arrangement, 74
catalogue entries, 73, 74
contents, 71-2
filing, 73
form, 71
position, 74
purpose, 71
responsibility, 72
revision and routine, 73-4
standards, 72
Visits to libraries
adults, 99-102
children, 87-98

Westminster public libraries, 38, 67
Wilson library bulletin, 131
Wire recorders, 80-81
Wording of notices, 39, 44

Yearbooks, *see* Annuals and
directories